the complete guide to

buying
property
in Italy

barbara mcmahon

KOGAN
PAGE

Publisher's note

Every possible effort has been made to ensure that the information contained in this book is accurate at the time of going to press, and the publisher and author cannot accept responsibility for any errors or omissions, however caused. No responsibility for loss or damage occasioned to any person acting, or refraining from action, as a result of the material in this publication can be accepted by the editor, the publisher or the author.

First published in Great Britain and the United States in 2004 by Kogan Page Limited

120 Pentonville Road
London N1 9JN
UK
www.kogan-page.co.uk

© Barbara McMahon, 2004

ISBN 0 7494 4151 8

British Library Cataloguing-in-Publication Data

A CIP record for this book is available from the British Library.

Typeset by Saxon Graphics Ltd, Derby
Printed and bound in Great Britain by Bell & Bain, Glasgow

Contents

Contents

Contents

Preface

So you are thinking about buying a property in Italy? Great choice. There is a wealth of different regions and climates to choose from and for its mix of art, history, culture, nature, good food and wine no other country, in my opinion, can beat it. Buying a house in Italy, however, is a huge financial and emotional investment and on the whole, people do not do enough research for such an important step in their lives. They are seduced by the dream of a private idyll among the olive groves and they rush into making a decision that they may come to regret. The most common mistakes are settling in the wrong area, choosing an unsuitable property, and getting out of your depth financially. This book will help you avoid these pitfalls but it will also encourage you to fulfil your dream. Regard it as your companion in this great adventure so that when you do buy an Italian home, whether it is a converted pigsty or a grand palazzo, you and your family will have happiness and peace of mind from your purchase for many years to come.

What do I know about buying property in Italy? Well, I am writing from my own home, an old stone farmhouse in Umbria. My husband and I spent months searching for the right house before we bought this property in 2001. The house was barely habitable when we first saw it – the animal *stalle* were still downstairs, the walls were black with grime, the only staircase was on the outside of the house and the adjoining 12 acres of land had been cruelly neglected, with grass waist-high in places and weeds running riot. We fell in love with it, nevertheless. The property had magnificent views of our local town, Orvieto, sitting atop its volcanic plug like some fairytale kingdom. There was an olive grove, cantina, pizza oven and caves studded with fossilized seashells, since the land had once been covered by the sea. Around us were fields fragrant with wild fennel, mint and thyme and there was a real sense that we could awaken this sleeping beauty and restore it to its former glory. It took a year of builders working flat out for the house to be brought back to order – we are still dealing with the garden – but the total cost of purchase and renovation was less than the price of a two bedroom apartment in central London. Shortly afterwards we took a deep breath, sold our home in London and moved here. It has been a very steep learning curve and all the challenges that we faced are still fresh in my mind, so I feel qualified to give advice to others. In this book I will tell you about the difficulties we encountered – you can learn from our mistakes!

Now that I am living in Italy my friends back home have an entirely unrealistic view of my day-to-day life. They think I spend mornings strolling dreamily through my olive grove in a flimsy chiffon dress or wandering down medieval streets with a straw basket under my arm, deciding what to buy for lunch. Of course there are many worthwhile moments in this new life – sitting in a piazza with a coffee and a newspaper, growing fruit and vegetables on our own land, or hopping on a train to go to Rome or Florence for the day. However, there is an enormous difference between being on holiday in Italy and actually living here. Settling down in a new country, learning the language, finding work, making friends and establishing your home and garden – it requires a lot of effort. There have been times when I have wandered down those medieval streets thinking, 'What the hell have we got ourselves into?'

This book will give you useful tips about how to settle in as painlessly as possible, whether you are thinking of living in Italy full-time or for only a few weeks a year. It will also give you practical advice on a diverse range of subjects such as learning the language, working and setting up a business and how to cut through all the red tape that threatens to strangle a foreigner in Italy. For those of you taking on the challenge of restoring an old house, you will find valuable information on choosing a professional building team and ensuring that the restoration is done to your taste and to your budget. Most of all, despite the moments when you will wonder if you should just go home, I hope this book gives you a sense of what fun it can be to build a new life in Italy.

A word about the property situation: prices are rising but there are still bargains to be found in every region, especially if you are prepared to renovate or build from scratch. There is always some *contadino* who wants to off-load his dilapidated house in the country. He does not see the beauty of its vaulted ceilings, terracotta floors and stone archways – he regards his old family home as a tumbledown wreck that has become too much trouble to maintain and he wants to move into modern accommodation, closer to a town or village. However, there are finite supplies of these types of old property, so you have to get moving.

To successfully buy a house in Italy you need enthusiasm and perseverance and you need to be willing to compromise, but there are huge rewards for those who do take the plunge. For many it will be not just a new holiday home but the first step in leaving the rat race behind and finding a more peaceful, tranquil way of life. I hope this personal account of how to buy a house in Italy, with all the information that I think a novice house-buyer needs, will help you in your search. *In bocca al lupo* – that means good luck!

John Howell's Top Tips

1. Plan before you go to look at property
Mortgage
UK or foreign mortgage? Get a preliminary mortgage offer before you go.

Deposit
Rather than pay any deposit by cheque, pay the money into our client account before you go. It is then very hard for the estate agent to persuade you to sign a contract without getting it checked first. Even "preliminary offers" should be checked before you sign them.

2. Take preliminary advice from your lawyer before you go
What are you going to use the property for?
Can the necessary permits be obtained?

Who should own the property?
If you put the property in the wrong names you will pay massively too much tax, both during your lifetime and on your death.

What you would like to happen to the property if you die?
In Italy you are not allowed to leave your property as you please.

Do you need a survey?

3. Always use an independent lawyer when you buy
Your lawyer will need to be familiar with the law of Italy and with the law of your own country.

Is the contract clear, legal and fair?

Does the property have all the necessary permissions & licences?

If you are buying before the property has been finished, how is your money protected?

Does the property have good title?

Is the property burdened by any debts?

4. Sort out the money
When you are sending Euros abroad there are various ways of converting and sending the money. Some are much better value and much cheaper than others.

5. Take out the right property insurance
Depending on how you intend to use your property you will need different types of insurance.

6. Make a local Will
This will save your heirs lots of money. Make a Will at the same time as you buy the house. If you don't you will forget.

1 Choosing your location and your property

You want to buy a property in Italy. The ideal scenario is that you have holidayed in one particular region for years and know the area well. You are in a café one morning having an espresso when a farmer mentions that his *mamma's* house is for sale. You go to see the house, realize it's a jewel of a property that would be snapped up in a second if it came onto the open market, agree a price and it's a happy ending for everyone. Sadly, this situation is unlikely to happen for most property hunters because you will be searching in areas of Italy that you do not know very well and will not have such local connections to call upon. How do you go about finding your dream home when you are not actually staying in Italy, have few or no leads to go on and do not speak the language?

First you must have a realistic idea of the practicalities involved and try to define what kind of property you are looking for. This will save a lot of time-wasting in the future. You need to think about why you want the house and how you are going to use it, at least in the short to medium term. Ask yourself the following questions.

How much do you want to spend?

Try to set a manageable budget – it's no use getting out of your financial depth and then worrying if you have done the right thing. I know one woman whose husband saw an Umbrian ruin advertised in a Sunday newspaper supplement. He took a plane out the following week and bought it. She burst into tears when she heard how much money he had committed to the project. Family holidays have had to go by the board ever since – much to the dismay of their teenage children – because all the family's spare cash and spare holiday time is being spent on restoring the house. Buying an Italian property shouldn't be such a drag on your finances that you have nightmares about how you are going to pay for it. Whatever your budget is, remember that buying costs in Italy are high. You will also have to set aside a contingency fund of about 20 per cent over and above any re-building costs to deal with extra expenses.

You could think about combining your money with family or friends – it might bring a much nicer house within your financial reach or enable you to get a swimming pool built more quickly. Sharing the financial responsibility with others is becoming increasingly popular in Italy since it enables groups of people to buy larger properties that remain on the market and then divide them. This may not be the solution for you but it does work for some people and it is worth thinking about.

Compare property prices in different areas of your chosen region and then zero in on an area that seems the best value. Your budget will obviously not go very far in cities like Rome, Florence or Venice. Rural properties are cheaper but it depends on proximity to local facilities, the size and condition of the house and its location. Once you have bought a house, the cost of living has to be taken into account – you will find it two or three times more expensive to live near Florence, for example, than you would in a small village in Puglia. Take all these factors into consideration when working out your budget.

Do you want rental income or is the property only for you and your family?

You don't need to have a huge Italian house in order to rent successfully – in fact, many rental agencies are actively looking for two to four bedroom properties to take onto their books. But if you want to make money from rental clients your house and its furnishings will have to have high-quality finishes and a swimming pool should be installed. These extra expenses will obviously have to be included in the overall sum that you plan to spend.

Will you go twice a year or every other weekend?

Budget air travel has transformed the cost of travelling to Italy but you need to look closely at the air timetables, the frequency of flights and whether they change during the winter months. There are year-round flights to all the big Italian cities but do the flights to the regional airports decrease in winter, when there are fewer tourists around? Do the arrival and take-off times suit your lifestyle? For example, Ryanair has numerous daily flights to Rome, but at the time of writing it has only one daily flight to Ancona, which returns to London late at night. Would this be a problem for you?

If you are planning to spend a lot of time at your home in Italy, especially going out for long weekends, you need to travel there and back with relative ease. Easy access also means thinking about the journey time once you land – a journey from the airport to your holiday home should be an absolute maximum of two hours; anything more is impractical.

Are you certain that this will only ever be a holiday home?

If you think you might live in Italy for good somewhere down the line you will have to consider being near schools, sources of employment or in the case of retiring, picking the right spot in which to spend the rest of your lives. For example, many small villages in Italy have been comprehensively depopulated – the young have all left to find work in the cities – and only old people live there now. These villages might not be the best places for foreign couples who want an active, sociable retirement. Similarly, if you are looking for a house in Italy with a view to moving your family there, you shouldn't choose a house halfway up a mountain. Your children will need the company of other young people.

What kind of climate do you want to live in?

You won't get sunshine and good weather all year round in Italy, but the climate is much more reliable in central and southern Italy. Verify local weather information for the area you have chosen on the Internet, with a site such as www.weather.com. In this way you can study the local weather patterns and get a much better idea of what living there would really be like.

If you choose a house near the mountains in Italy, for example, it will have its own microclimate and will not be as sunny and warm in summer as you expect and there will be blizzards in winter. Where I live it is extremely hot in summer, cold and rainy in winter – this year temperatures in Umbria got down to –6°C – and spring always arrives much later than in the UK so Easter can be quite chilly. If you are a skier and want snow in the winter there are many different types of skiing areas, ranging from those with only the most basic facilities to very sophisticated resorts. It's a good excuse to go out for long weekends to scout around.

Do you want to have access to the sea or are you content to be inland?

It's wonderful to have a house by the sea or near to a marina but such properties will be more expensive. The cost of living is likely to be higher too since coastal resorts cater to tourists, therefore eating out and other entertainments will be pricier.

What size of house?

Many foreigners make the mistake of buying Italian houses that are too big. They look at an enormous old farmhouse and fall for it because they could never afford a property of the same size back in their home country. So they go ahead and buy it and then realize what they have let themselves in for. Remember that these huge properties cost small fortunes to renovate – at least two to three times the purchase price – and they are extremely expensive to furnish and to heat in winter. Maintenance costs can be a huge worry. Think about how many spare bedrooms you need. Do you really want to have lots of guests? You may end up feeling that you are running a small hotel, especially in the summer months. You might instead prefer to buy a smaller property near a town with hotel or *agriturismo* accommodation so that guests can put themselves up.

Do you want to move into a house that is already habitable or to restore a ruin?

Good builders in Italy – those with proven track records of restoring old houses – are in high demand and you may have to wait many months for these builders to become available. Planning permission to convert old properties can also take up to a year, depending on which region you are in. Therefore, if you choose a ruin, it could be at least two years before you can actually live in your house and you would have to rent a property in the meantime or stay in hotel or *agriturismo* accommodation. Moving into a house that is already habitable, even if there is some redecorating to do, means you can start your Italian adventure straight away.

Will your regular guests – like elderly parents and teenage children – be able to drive?

If not, you should try to find a house within easy distance of a train or bus station or you will find that you are forever thrashing down the *autostrada* to pick up people from the airport. Being an unpaid taxi service becomes very irritating after a while.

Do you want to be way out in the country or near to a town or village?

You will get a cheaper property in a rural area, but make sure it is not too far away from everything – isolation can pall very quickly. Houses at bargain prices can be found but this may be because there are few facilities nearby – a single bar with a pinball table, for example, and a lone grocery store. Part of the joy of living in Italy is going to restaurants, cafes, shops and local markets, so you want to be within easy reach of these things, not stuck with a tedious car journey every day. You also have to think about winter – would you need a 4x4 vehicle if you were stuck up a dirt track somewhere? Consider the security aspect. Houses in remote rural areas – particularly if it is known that they are owned by foreigners and not inhabited all year round – are vulnerable to burglaries. You may feel safer being in the countryside if you have neighbours nearby who will notice if there are strangers lurking around. An inquisitive neighbour can be very effective in discouraging burglaries.

How much land do you want?

Are you looking for several hectares with olive groves and vines or just a small manageable garden? (Note: land in Italy is usually measured in hectares. One hectare is 2.47 acres or 10,000 sq metres.) Part of the Italian dream, of course, is having some land or a beautiful garden. But don't get carried away by thoughts of buying up a whole hillside, because looking after land is hard work and very expensive. We have 5 hectares (approx 12 acres) and it is a huge amount of effort in summer watering every-thing, especially when there is a drought and you cannot spare enough water to keep the plants alive. In winter heavy rain can lead to landslides and other disasters and so a lot of our time is spent on maintenance. We have also had to buy a lot of serious farm equipment: you cannot get away with a little lawn-mower from B & Q and a spade and shovel in this kind of terrain. Similarly, an olive grove or a vineyard is a luxury but it is also a huge responsibility and you are unlikely to make much, if any, money from it.

Do you want to be in a tourist-oriented area?

You may feel less out of place in a city or resort where you can socialize with other English speakers. The regions of Italy where there are the biggest expatriate populations are Tuscany, Umbria, Lazio, Liguria, Le Marche, Lombardy, Campania and Sicily.

How important is a swimming pool?

Check the situation in your chosen area – there are many beautiful houses to restore in the national parks of Italy, but permission for swimming pools is restricted or forbidden because it ruins the natural beauty of the area.

Getting started

You should also sit down with members of your family and ask each of them to visualize their ideal house in Italy. This can be very illuminating. There is likely to be general agreement about such things as the minimum number of bedrooms required and the importance of a swimming pool, but you may find that different members of the family have conflicting and unrealistic ideals of what you can afford. It is best to get all this out in the open at the very beginning. Now draw up another wish list incorporating your family's essential requirements.

You are beginning to build up a picture of the kind of Italian property that you want. You should also have done your research on the region of Italy where you will be house hunting. Narrow your focus on a particular part of your chosen region: you cannot efficiently search the whole of Tuscany, for example, or the whole of Liguria unless you are going to take weeks or months off work.

With your budget and location in mind, get on to the Internet and type the phrase 'property for sale in...' whatever region of Italy you have chosen. This will bring up a selection of Web sites for foreign house hunters and you can begin to trawl through them, getting a feel for what is available and at what cost. There will be a mix of Italian and English-language Web sites – don't be put off by the ones you do not understand. You can still look at pictures of ruined farmhouses, derelict monasteries and uninhabited *castelli* and work out how much they cost.

What you will not see are the settings of these properties, the reason why some of them are being advertised at attractive prices. They will fail to show the monstrous electricity pylon next to a house, the *autostrada* running through the bottom of the valley, or the foul-smelling battery farm in the next field. Some estate agents keep pictures on their Web sites of houses that have long since been sold – this is to attract buyers who will then be shown the less attractive properties that are left. I am alerting you to these practices simply to forewarn you, because when I first started searching I fully expected to be shown properties that I had seen on Web sites and I discovered that either the descriptions were way off the mark or the nice ones had already been sold.

Nevertheless, searching on the Internet is a very good first step to getting yourself attuned to the market in your particular area – it's also great fun to do and I certainly spent hours snooping away very happily. If you have friends or family who have already bought a house in Italy, quiz them about their experiences and ask if they have any contacts you could use. You should also look at the property sections of the Sunday newspaper supplements, which often publish articles about moving to Italy, as well as advertisements about private sales or sales through estate agencies. In newsagents stores in your chosen area or at newsstands at the airport, you will find specialist Italian publications such as *Ville e Casali*. These types of magazine are very useful for seeing what properties are out there and you will drool at how beautiful some of the properties are – something to aspire to! *Italy* magazine (see www.italymag.co.uk) is published in Britain and is another good resource. It has a range of estate agency adverts to set you on your way.

2 The regions and provinces of Italy

Abruzzo – L'Aquila
  Chieti
  Pescara
  Teramo
Basilicata – Potenza
  Matera
Calabria – Reggio di Calabria
  Catanzaro
  Cosenza
  Crotone
  Vibo Valentia
Campania – Napoli
  Avellino
  Benevento
  Caserta
  Salerno
Emilia-Romagna – Bologna
  Ferrara
  Forli-Cesena
  Modena
  Parma
  Piacenza
  Ravenna
  Reggio nell'Emilia
  Rimini
Friuli-Venezia Giulia – Trieste
  Gorizia
  Pordenone
  Udine
Lazio – Roma
  Frosinone
  Latina
  Rieti
  Viterbo
Marche – Ancona
  Ascoli Piceno
  Macerata
  Pesaro e Urbino

Liguria – Genova
  Imperia
  La Spezia
  Savona
Lombardia – Milano
  Bergamo
  Brescia
  Como
  Cremona
  Lecco
  Lodi
  Mantova
  Pavia
  Sondrio
  Varese
Molise – Campobasso
  Isernia
Piemonte – Torino
  Alessandria
  Asti
  Biella
  Cuneo
  Novara
  Verbano-Cusio-Ossola
  Vercelli
Puglia – Bari
  Brindisi
  Foggia
  Lecce
  Taranto
Sardegna – Cagliari
  Nuoro
  Oristano
  Sassari
Sicilia – Palermo
  Agrigento
  Caltanissetta
  Catania

Enna

Messina

Ragusa

Siracusa

Trapani

Trentino-Alto Adige – Trento

Bolzano-Bozen

Toscana – Firenze

Arezzo

Grosseto

Livorno

Lucca

Massa-Carrara

Pisa

Pistoia

Prato

Siena

Umbria – Perugia

Terni

Valle d'Aosta – Valle d'Aosta

Veneto – Venezia

Belluno

Padova

Rovigo

Treviso

Verona

Vicenza

Italy is a peninsula situated in southern Europe, with 7,375 kilometres of coastline. It has a population of 58 million people, borders Austria, France, Slovenia and Switzerland, and includes the Vatican City, the small republic of San Marino and the islands of Sicily and Sardinia. Italy became a unified country in 1860; before that date it was a group of republics. Italy's climate is predominantly Mediterranean, Alpine in the far north, hot and dry in the south. Italian is the official language with a minority of the population speaking French in the Valle D'Aosta, German in Trentino-Alto Adige and Slovene in Trieste. The principal cities are Rome (population 2.7 million), Milan (1.3 million), Naples (1 million) and Turin (900,000).

The country's main industries are tourism, textiles, clothing and ceramics, car manufacturing, iron and steel production, chemicals, engineering products and production of food, wine and tobacco. Some 53 per cent of Italian exports go to European Union countries – around 7 per cent to Britain. Most industrial companies are concentrated in the north of the country, which is therefore more densely populated and economically sound than the less developed south. At the time of writing, the unemployment rate in Italy was 9 per cent with pockets of much higher unemployment in the south. Inflation has remained relatively stable at around 2.7 per cent.

Italy is an artistic treasure house, blessed with some of the finest art collections and architecture in the world as well as landscapes to swoon over. Tourism is its main industry. Millions of foreigners visit every year and some 60 per cent of the working population is connected to the service sector. Italy is one of the biggest wine-producing countries in the world. Once regarded as a mass producer of low-quality wine, there has been a renaissance in Italian winemaking in recent years and the country now has an excellent worldwide reputation for individuality and quality.

There are 20 regions – Abruzzo, Basilicata, Calabria, Campania, Emilia-Romagna, Friuli-Venezia Giulia, Lazio, Liguria, Lombardy, Marche, Molise, Piedmont, Puglia, Sardinia, Sicily, Trentino-Alto Adige, Tuscany, Umbria, Valle D'Aosta and Veneto – that are described below. Italy has 103 provinces and 8,101 municipal councils. All population figures given below are according to the last census.

Abruzzo

Abruzzo, with its choice of mountains or coastline, stretches from the Apennines to the Adriatic Sea and borders Marche, Lazio and Molise. The population of the region is 1,232,454 people and there are four provinces: L'Aquila, Chieti, Pescara and Teramo. L'Aquila is the capital although Pescara is also strategically important with more than 100,000 inhabitants, its own airport and marina. Other significant towns are Atri, Penne, Sulmona and Chieti. Some 65 per cent of the region is mountainous – the highest peaks of the Apennines are here – and the ski season usually lasts till April.

Abruzzo is also famous for its national parks – Parco Gran Sasso Monti della Laga, Parco Nazionale D'Abruzzo, Parco Nazionale della Maiella and Parco Velino Sirente – and nature lovers will find plenty to do in these well-maintained nature reserves. You can trek, camp, go horse riding or mountain-biking or simply appreciate the huge variety of plants, trees, flowers and wildlife on display. You may spot grey wolf, the Marsican bear or wild eagles in the 44,000 hectare *Parco Nazionale D'Abruzzo*.

There are good beaches along the coast from Martinsicuro to Vasto, and elsewhere in the region you will find castles and fortified hill villages. The university capital of L'Aquila (which means eagle) has many noteworthy museums, churches and a wonderful castle.

Summers are warm all over the region while winters next to the sea are mild and it is very cold in the mountains – often below freezing.

Abruzzo's economy is based on agriculture – wheat, corn, olives, grapes, barley, beans, oregano and potatoes are all grown here as well as strawberries, blueberries, mulberries, cherries and raspberries. At Altopiano di Navelli, saffron (*Crocus Sativus*) is grown and exported worldwide, liquorice is grown in Atri, and Santo Stefano di Sessanio is famous for its lentils and orzo. The region also has a long tradition of raising sheep, goats and cattle.

Pescara and Chieti are the two most industrialized cities in Abruzzo with textiles, furniture and new technology the main sources of employment. Some of Italy's best dried pasta is made in Abruzzo.

Abruzzo has not traditionally been popular with foreign property buyers but there has been significant interest shown in the last couple of years, partly due to the daily flights to Pescara by Ryanair, which makes it easier and cheaper to reach the area. Local estate agents claim this is the last area in central Italy where property is still undervalued. A semi-detached stone house in a rural area starts at 20,000 euros plus restoration costs; a good detached house to restore, with views of the mountains and the sea, will be approximately 100,000 euros upwards. Castles and former *agriturismos* are also for sale – 500,000 euros upwards. Property prices are higher along the coast.

UK travel links

Pescara is an international airport with connections to Brussels, Frankfurt and London. Ryanair flies daily to Pescara from London Stansted.

Other travel information

Rail

Rome – L'Aquila	3.30 hours
Rome – Chieti	3.45 hours
Rome – Teramo	5.30 hours
Rome – Pescara	3.45 hours

Road

Abruzzo has good communication with Rome on the A24 and A25 *autostradas* and the A14 runs north to south along the coast.

Rome – Pescara   205kms, 2.30 hours

Basilicata

Basilicata, also known as Lucania, has two coastlines – the Ionian to the south-east and the Tyrrhenian to the south-west. In Italy's deep south, with a population of 568,967, its regions are called Potenza and Matera. Potenza is also the main town and is the highest regional capital of Italy, standing at 819 metres. Matera has been declared a World Heritage site because of its ancient cave-houses dug out of rock, and is now a major tourist attraction. Clear waters and fine, golden sand mean the beaches are a joy and Maratea, Pisticci, Policoro, Nova Siri and Scanzano Jonico are all popular resorts, mostly with Italians who come down from the north seeking better weather. Nature lovers will find plenty to see and do in Pollino National Park. Remains of the Greek era can be found in Metaponto, while Roman ruins can be seen in Venosa. There is a wealth of museums with important prehistoric and Roman relics, as well as important medieval art. Expect hot weather in summer and mild winters in Basilicata. Rainfall is variable but there is never enough and this region is known for its arid, scorched landscape.

Basilicata was once one of the poorest regions of Italy but is now enjoying a renaissance in its fortunes, thanks partly to better state funding. Matera has a thriving textile industry and thousands of local people are employed in furniture production. Agriculture remains an important part of the economy and olive oil, olives, almonds and tomatoes are exported, as well as the famous *lucanica* sausage. Young people who used to go abroad to seek their fortunes are now staying put and opening businesses, giving the area a vibrant, lively feel. However, this region is not of huge interest to foreign property buyers since direct travel links are difficult.

UK travel links

Basilicata has no airports with direct links to the UK. Neighbouring regions Puglia and Campania have airports with direct flights to the UK. In Puglia, Bari has scheduled direct flights to London:

Bari	London Stansted	Ryanair
	London Gatwick	BA

In Campania, Naples is a busy international airport served by many flights to the UK (S = Summer only):

Naples	Birmingham	(S) Britannia, Air 2000
	Bristol	(S) Britannia, Air 2000
	East Midlands	(S) Air 2000
	Glasgow	(S) Britannia
	London Stansted	easyJet
	London Gatwick	BA, (S) Britannia, Air 2000, Monarch
	Luton	(S) Britannia
	Manchester	(S) Air 2000, Britannia

Other travel information

Rail

Rome – Potenza	5 hours

Road

Rome – Potenza	370 kms, 3.45 hours

Calabria

This region, which has a population of 1,945,130, forms the toe of Italy's boot and is in the far south-west, with coastlines on the Tyrrhenian and Ionian seas. The capital and principal province is Catanzaro and other provinces are Reggio di Calabria, Cosenza, Crotone and Vibo Valentia. Calabria has a largely inaccessible mountainous interior but it has wonderful coastlines with unspoilt beaches and crystal clear water. Calabria has been described as being 'a bit rough at the edges', with most foreigners regarding it only as a region to drive through to get to Sicily. As one of the poorest regions, it has suffered from high employment and a high crime rate. However, the people are warm and hospitable and Calabria has a rich architectural heritage, with many Roman and Greek ruins. The area around the coastal town of Tropea is particularly developed and is popular with Italian and German holidaymakers. The climate is very hot in summer and mild in winter. Again, this area of Italy does not excite huge interest among foreign property buyers because transport links are difficult. A holiday apartment with views of the sea and two bedrooms would cost approx 80,000 euros, while a new-build house next to the sea, with three bedrooms, can be found for 130,000 euros, although it will need updating.

UK travel links

Reggio di Calabria has no scheduled direct flights to the UK. The nearest airport with direct connections to the UK is Palermo in Sicily, which is 230 kms away.

Other travel information

Rail

Rome – Catanzaro	6 hours
Rome – Cosenza	5 hours
Rome – Reggio di Calabria	6.15 hours

Road

The principal motorway is the A3 Salerno-Reggio Calabria *autostrada*.

Rome – Reggio-Calabria   710 kms, 6.50 hours
Rome – Catanzaro   620 kms, 6.05 hours

Campania

Campania, with a population of 5,642,397, is also known as the Neapolitan Riviera and in this region you will find one of the finest coastlines in Italy – the famous Amalfi coast. Sorrento, Positano, Ravello and Amalfi are all in this area and ferries are available to the islands of Capri and Ischia. Naples, Avellino, Benevento, Caserta and Salerno are the five provinces and Naples, which stands in the shadow of the volcano Vesuvius, is the capital city. Because of its natural beauty and extraordinary architectural ruins – Pompeii, Herculaneum and the Phlegrean Fields to name a few – this region is a magnet for tourists. But Campania also has fertile farmland and a mountainous interior that is worth exploring.

One of Italy's most southern regions, Campania enjoys very warm summers and mild winters. Resorts are generally open April to October and some re-open for Christmas and New Year before closing down again. Sorrento and towns on the Amalfi coast generally remain open all year round.

Property prices depend on where you want to be – on the Amalfi coast they are astronomical. A tiny 90 sq metre apartment with a terrace costs 450,000 euros. Houses with sea views and gardens are well over a million euros. Properties on Capri and Ischia are extremely difficult to find and expensive when you do. Away from the coast, you can find a small new-build house in the countryside for 90,000 euros, a new-build villa on three floors – with one floor still to complete – for 184,000 euros and in the town of Salerno a three bedroom, two bathroom apartment will cost 372,000 euros.

UK travel links

British Airways and easyJet have direct daily flights to Naples. In the summer, Naples is served by charter flights from Manchester, Birmingham and Bristol (S = Summer only):

Naples		
	Birmingham	(S) Britannia, Air 2000
	Bristol	(S) Britannia, Air 2000
	East Midlands	(S) Air 2000
	Glasgow	(S) Britannia
	London Stansted	easyJet
	London Gatwick	BA, Alitalia, (S) Britannia, Air 2000, Monarch
	Luton	(S) Britannia
	Manchester	(S) Air 2000, Britannia

Other travel information

Rail

Rome – Avellino	3.30 hours
Rome – Benevento	0.20 hours
Rome – Caserta	1.40 hours
Rome – Naples	1.45 hours
Rome – Salerno	2.30 hours

Road

The region is well-served by three major *autostradas*, A1, A16 and A3.

Rome – Naples	230 kms, 2.25 hours
Rome – Salerno	270 kms, 2.50 hours

Emilia-Romagna

The regions of Emilia and Romagna were unified in 1946 and the territory is defined by the flat, sandy beaches of the Adriatic Riviera and the imposing Apennines. The capital is Bologna, which has the oldest university in Italy (est. 1088) and outstanding medieval piazzas and porticos. The region has a population of 4,035,131 and the provinces are Bologna, Ferrara, Forli-Cesena, Modena, Parma, Piacenza, Ravenna, Reggio nell'Emilia and Rimini. This region is renowned for its gastronomic pleasures – this is the home of Parma ham, Parmigiano Reggiano and Balsamic vinegar – and many of Italy's best restaurants are in Bologna or the surrounding areas. Summers are warm and humid and winters are cold, rainy and foggy. Seaside resorts like Rimini close from October to April but winter sports enthusiasts will find plenty of skiing in high altitude resorts such as Corno alle Scale, Sestola, Cerreto, Schia, Fanano and Montecreto. Salsomaggiore is the region's best-known spa.

The area around Bologna is one of the wealthiest in Italy and property is better value if you go further away from the main cities. A small unrestored stone house of 130 sq metres with a garden and panoramic views of the Apennines is 60,000 euros, a group of farm buildings to restore, with six hectares of land and proximity to the main ski resorts, is 160,000 euros, while a brand-new, one bedroom apartment costs around 95,000 euros.

UK travel links

British Airways has direct daily flights from Gatwick to Bologna, and Ryanair flies daily to Bologna Forli (approx 40 miles distant from Bologna). During the summer Rimini has its own airport, receiving mostly charter flights from London and Manchester (S = Summer only):

Bologna (Forli)	London Stansted	Ryanair, easyJet
Bologna	London Gatwick	BA
Rimini	London Stansted	(S) Charter
	Manchester	(S) MyTravel

Other travel information

Rail

Rome – Bologna	2.40 hours
Rome – Ferrara	3.15 hours
Rome – Forli	3.30 hours
Rome – Modena	3.15 hours
Rome – Parma	3.30 hours
Rome – Piacenza	4.10 hours
Rome – Ravenna	4.30 hours

Road

This region is crisscrossed by major *autostradas*. The A1 heads south to Florence and north-west to Milan. The A13 goes to Padova and Venice, and the A14 goes to Ravenna and Rimini.

Rome – Bologna	388 kms, 4.05 hours
Rome – Parma	467 kms, 4.45 hours
Rome – Ravenna	388 kms, 4.40 hours

Friuli-Venezia Giulia

This fascinating region borders Slovenia and Austria, has a population of 1,179,188, and is one of the most cosmopolitan parts of Italy. The capital is Trieste, the largest port on the Adriatic, where Slovene is also spoken. There is also widespread use of the local dialect Friulian. The other provinces are Udine, Gorizia, and Pordenone. This region remains one of the most undiscovered in Italy but it has many attractions – beautiful beaches on the Adriatic, Alpine scenery and warm Friulian hospitality. FVG produces some of Italy's finest wines and the famous ham is produced in San Daniele. Cuisine reflects the region's Italian, German and Slavic influences. The climate is generally temperate but the region can be hit by thunderstorms and hailstorms during the summer months. Winters are cold and damp. The 'bora' is a north-easterly wind of 150km per hour that can strike Trieste and its environs. Property prices for holiday homes are reasonable, with an apartment in a shared chalet building in the mountains costing upwards of 90,000 euros.

UK travel links

Trieste has direct flights on Ryanair to Stansted. The area is mainly served by Venice's two airports (see Venice) (S = Summer only):

Trieste	London Stansted	Ryanair
Venice (Marco Polo)	Bristol	easyJet, (S) Charter
	Birmingham	BA, BMI Baby, (S) Monarch
	Dublin	Aer Lingus
	East Midlands	easyJet
	London Gatwick	BA, (S) Monarch
	London Heathrow	BMI
	London Stansted	easyJet, Ryanair
	Manchester	BA, (S) Britannia, Astraeus, Monarch, MyTravel
Venice (Treviso)	London Stansted	Ryanair

Other travel information

Rail

Rome – Gorizia	7.01 hours
Rome – Pordenone	5.48 hours
Rome – Trieste	6.30 hours
Rome – Udine	7.04 hours

Road

Excellent road links into Austria on the A23 and the A4 connects with Venice, Padova, etc.

Rome – Trieste   680 kms, 6 hours 40
Rome – Gorizia   656 kms, 6 hours 25

Lazio

All roads lead to Rome and as a result, the rest of this region tends to be overlooked. But there are lots of interesting medieval towns and villages with many reminders of Roman and Etruscan civilizations. Lazio has a population of 4,843,576, and its provinces are Rome, Frosinone, Latina, Rieti and Viterbo. Holiday resorts have sprung up around volcanic lakes such as Bracciano and many Romans either commute or have bought second homes in the countryside. Lazio has resorts along a stretch of the Tyrhennian Sea and it also encompasses the western buttresses of the Apennines. The climate is warm in summer and mild and rainy in winter.

There is a wide range of property available in this part of central Italy and many foreign buyers who find houses in Umbria and Tuscany too expensive are purchasing here. An apartment in one of the picturesque towns is an option – a three bedroom apartment to restore in historic Civitella D'Agliano is 90,000 euros while a stone farmhouse to restore in the countryside, with a small garden, is an average 150,000 euros. A church and an un-restored hilltop farmhouse, with 2.5 hectares of land, is 500,000 euros, while a five bedroom house in a seaside area such as Santa Severa will be over half a million euros.

UK travel links

British Airways has daily direct flights to Rome Fiumicino from London (Gatwick and Heathrow), Birmingham and Manchester. Alitalia flies from

London Heathrow and London Gatwick. Alitalia also flies direct from Dublin to Fiumicino. Rome's smaller airport Ciampino has daily direct flights by Ryanair and easyJet from Stansted and in summer, charter flights from Glasgow with Globespan (S = Summer only):

Rome (Fiumicino)	Birmingham	BA
	Cork	Aer Lingus
	Dublin	Alitalia
	Edinburgh	(S) BA
	London Gatwick	BA, Alitalia
	London Heathrow	BA, Alitalia
	Manchester	BA
Rome (Ciampino)	London Stansted	Ryanair, easyJet
	Edinburgh	(S) FlyGlobespan
	Glasgow	(S) FlyGlobespan

Other travel information

Rail

Rome – Latina	0.28 hours
Rome – Rieti	1.52 hours
Rome – Viterbo	1.42 hours

Road

Rome – Viterbo	83kms, 1.25 hours
Rome – Rieti	86 kms, 1.25 hours

Liguria

Liguria faces the Tyrrhenian Sea in an arc, with the Gulf of Genoa in the centre. The region is divided into two sections: the Riviera di Ponente to the west, from Ventimiglia to Genoa, and the Riviera di Levante to the east, from Genoa to La Spezia. Liguria has a population of 1,567,889 and the capital of the region is Genoa. The other provinces are La Spezia, Savona and Imperia. This region is better known as the Italian Riviera and tourism is the main source of employment here. Liguria enjoys a mild, temperate climate all year round. Alassio, San Remo, Portofino and the area known as *Le Cinque Terre* (the Five Lands) are the most popular parts of this region. The coastal strip in Liguria can be less than 10 kilometres deep before rising to 500 or 600 metres, so houses are built at dizzy heights and seem to cling on to the cliffside – these kinds of properties have fabulous views but are very exposed to the vagaries of the weather. If you are looking for property don't bother with Portofino unless you are extremely rich. This picture-postcard port is a playground for the very wealthy and a plot of land, if you can find it, will cost well over a million euros – not to mention the cost of building a new house. Villas on the cliffside are also scarce and ruinously expensive. A four bedroom house with one acre of land in *Le Cinque Terre* will cost 600,000 euros. A two bedroom apartment in a new-build block facing the sea will cost 400,000 euros. Houses to restore in the Imperia area are being advertised at 30,000–300,000 euros.

UK travel links

Genoa has daily flights with British Airways from London Gatwick and Ryanair from London Stansted. Pisa airport in Tuscany, to the south of Liguria, is served by British Airways from London Gatwick and Ryanair from Stansted. In the summer there are charter flights from Leeds/Bradford, Manchester, East Midlands and Bristol:

Genoa	London Gatwick	BA
	London Stansted	Ryanair

Other travel information

Rail

Rome – Genoa	5.03 hours
Rome – Imperia	7.05 hours
Rome – La Spezia	3.55 hours
Rome – Savona	5.58 hours

Road

Calais to Genoa via the Mont Blanc tunnel is approx 12 hours. Major *autostradas* are A6, A7, A10, A12 and A26. The A10 heads west from Genoa towards Monte Carlo, the A6 links Liguria with Turin and the Alps, the A26 heads north towards Switzerland, the A7 links Genoa with Milan and the A12 hugs the coast, heading south to Pisa, Livorno and Tuscany.

Rome – Genoa	514 kms, 5.10 hours
Rome – La Spezia	430 kms, 4.20 hours

Lombardy (Lombardia)

Fashionable Milan with its elegant and expensive shopping streets and the magnificent lakes of Como and Garda sum up this northern region, which sits in the main part of the Po Valley and borders Switzerland. Lombardy has a population of 8,967,864. Milan, the heart of Italy's fashion industry, is the capital and other provinces are Bergamo, Brescia, Como, Cremona, Lecco, Lodi, Mantova, Varese, Pavia and Sondrio. Lake Como is one of Europe's deepest lakes and on its banks are opulent villas and gorgeous gardens owned by some of the richest people in Europe. The Hollywood actor George Clooney has bought a spectacular villa here. Lake Garda is similarly spectacular and there are enchanting lake towns such as Limone sul Garda and

Desenzano. The climate around the lakes is a microclimate so the weather is mild in winter while there is good skiing in resorts such as Valsassina, Valvarrone and Valcavargna. An apartment in Milan is probably comparable in price to London – a two bedroom apartment in a good area of the city will cost 300,000 euros. Many Milanese are buying properties in the environs of Milan, near towns such as Stresa and Verbania, in order to commute, so property is expensive here. A one bedroom apartment with views of Lake Como will cost 100,000 euros while a new-build two bedroom villa near the lakes will cost 275,000 euros.

UK travel links

Milan Linate airport is served by British Airways, BMI, Alitalia and easyJet. Ryanair flies to Milan-Bergamo, which is also served by BMI Baby from Cardiff. Malpensa is the international airport with British Airways and Alitalia flying direct flights from London and Manchester. BA also flies from Birmingham to Malpensa. FlyBe goes from Birmingham to Milan-Bergamo. Aer Lingus and Alitalia fly from Dublin. ChannelExpress flies from Leeds/Bradford. BMI Baby flies from East Midlands and FlyBe flies from Southampton (S = Summer only):

Milan Bergamo	Cardiff	BMI Baby
	Glasgow-Prestwick	Ryanair
	London Stansted	Ryanair
Milan Linate	London Heathrow	BA, BMI, Alitalia
	London Gatwick	easyJet
	London Stansted	easyJet
Milan Malpensa	Birmingham	BA, FlyBe
	Cork	Aer Lingus
	Dublin	Aer Lingus, Alitalia
	East Midlands	BMI Baby
	Edinburgh	Duo Airlines
	Leeds/Bradford	Channel Express
	London Heathrow	BA, Alitalia
	Manchester	(S) BA, Charter, Alitalia
	Southampton	FlyBe

Other travel information

Rail

Rome – Bergamo	5.38 hours
Rome – Brescia	5.01 hours
Rome – Como	5.16 hours
Rome – Cremona	4.43 hours
Rome – Mantova	4.38 hours
Rome – Milan	4.30 hours
Rome – Pavia	5.13 hours
Rome – Sondrio	6.50 hours
Rome – Varese	6.01 hours

Road

Milan is the communications hub of northern Italy and therefore has excellent road and rail connections to all parts of Italy and Europe.

Rome – Milan	585 kms, 5.50 hours
Rome – Como	634 kms, 6.15 hours
Rome – Bergamo	610 kms, 6 hours

Marche

This region lies on the eastern side of central Italy, between the Adriatic sea and the Apennines. It borders Emilia-Romagna to the north, Tuscany and Umbria to the west and Abruzzo and Lazio to the south. The hilltop republic of San Marino is in the north. It has a population of 1,468,526 and its provinces are Ancona, Ascoli Piceno, Macerata and Pesaro-Urbino.

Like its neighbours Tuscany and Umbria, Marche is essentially hilly and is full of attractive villages, vine-covered hills and important artistic works. The capital is Ancona. Marche's coastline is over 180kms long with two types of beach resort. San Benedetto del Tronto, Pesaro, Senigallia and Gabicce Mare all have wide, sandy beaches but they are chock-full of people and can be quite flat and uninteresting. There are smaller resorts such as Portonovo, Sirolo and Numana, some of which have spectacular beaches framed by impressive cliffs. The Sibillini national park is the region's biggest and Monte Vettore in the highest mountain in the region. Weather is generally warm in summer but a few degrees cooler than in Tuscany or Umbria. Winters are cold with snow in mountainous areas, mild by the sea and generally rainy in February and March.

Estate agents have been calling Marche the new Tuscany or Umbria for several years and this picturesque part of Italy is now extremely popular with foreign property buyers. Property prices continue to rise but it is still possible to find attractive farmhouses to restore. The price you will have to pay will depend on how canny the vendor is. Some Marchegiani have not yet realized that Marche is one of the hottest property areas in Italy and are happy to off-load their unwanted house in the country for 30,000 euros. However, if you find the property through an agent the vendor is more likely to be clued up on its potential value. In this case, a stone house in a good area will cost 80,000 euros upwards plus restoration costs.

UK travel links

Ancona has a daily direct flight by Ryanair from Stansted. The north of Marche can also be accessed from Rimini, which has charter flights in the summer (S = Summer only):

Ancona	London Stansted	Ryanair
Rimini	London Stansted	(S) Charter
	Manchester	(S) MyTravel

Other travel information

Rail

Rome – Ancona	3.08 hours
Rome – Ascoli Piceno	5.53 hours
Rome – Macerata	3.38 hours

Road

Travelling east to west, traversing the Apennines, can be slow because there are few fast roads. The only major *autostrada* is the A14, which runs along the Adriatic coast.

Rome – Ancona	307 kms, 3.20 hours
Rome – Macerata	300 kms, 3.15 hours
Rome – Ascoli Piceno	216 kms, 2.35 hours

Molise

Until 1963, Molise was part of Abruzzo and this is a tiny territory – only 550 sq miles and with a population of 300,143 – of hills and mountains facing the Adriatic Sea. The capital is Campobasso and the other main province is Isernia. Agriculture and raising sheep, goats and cattle are the main sources of income. Wheat, corn, potatoes, tomatoes, fava beans and lentils are grown and pasta, black truffles and olive oil are exported all over the world.

Tourism has not really been developed here so there are limited facilities and few foreigners have thought about buying property here. The Molisano are hugely influenced in language, tradition and customs by their neighbours across the Adriatic in Croatia and Albania and there is a sizeable Albanian-speaking community here, largely centred on the town of Ururi. Molise, which has been struck by many earthquakes, remains one of the poorest and least developed regions of Italy.

UK travel links

There are no direct flights to and from the UK. See Naples or Pescara airports for the nearest direct flights.

Other travel information

Rail

Rome – Campobasso	3.15 hours
Rome – Isernia	2.14 hours

Road

Rome – Campo Basso	605 kms, 6 hours
Rome – Isernia	187 kms, 2.20 hours

Piedmont (Piemonte)

Piemonte means foot of the mountains and refers to the fact that Piedmont sits at the foot of the Alps. The region is bordered by France in the west, Switzerland and Valle D'Aosta in the north, Lombardy and Emila-Romagna in the east and Liguria in the south. It has a population of 4,184,901 and its provinces are Turin, Alessandria, Asti, Biella, Cuneo, Novara and Verbenio-Cusio-Ossola. This is one of Italy's most important wine-producing regions – rich reds such as Barolo, Nebbiolo and Barbaresco come from here and sparkling Asti Spumante and vermouth are also produced locally. Piedmont is also the source of white truffles – much in demand all over the world. The mighty Po River has its source here and Lake Maggiore and Lake Orta are popular spots for tourists.

Turin, which is a big and sprawling city, is the heart of Italy's car-manufacturing business – the Fiat car company was established in 1899 – and there is also a large chemical industry here. It will host the Winter Olympics in 2006. In the interior of Piedmont, the region is noted for its historic castles set amid mountain scenery and its vineyards. Piedmont has a continental climate with warm, dry summers and cold winters.

Most second-home buyers in Piedmont want to be near the lakes or the mountains. A one bedroom apartment with views of Lake Maggiore costs approx 100,000 euros, a new three bedroom detached house with garden and lake views is 300,000 euros. In the Langhe district a small semi-detached house in the centre of a village, with views of the Alps, is 40,000 euros, while a stone-built, fully restored villa with three bedrooms, swimming pool and 10 hectares of land is around 775,000 euros.

UK travel links

Fly from Turin, Genoa or Milan. Turin has daily flights by Ryanair from Stansted (S = Summer only):

Turin	London Gatwick	(S) Air 2000
	London Stansted	Ryanair
	Manchester	(S) Air 2000
Genoa	London Gatwick	BA
	London Stansted	Ryanair
Milan Bergamo	Cardiff	BMI Baby
	London Stansted	Ryanair
Milan Linate	London Heathrow	BA, BMI, Alitalia
	London Gatwick	easyJet
	London Stansted	easyJet
Milan Malpensa	Birmingham	BA, FlyBe
	Cork	Aer Lingus
	Dublin	Aer Lingus, Alitalia
	East Midlands	BMI Baby

Leeds/Bradford	Channel Express
London Heathrow	BA, Alitalia
Manchester	(S) BA, Charter
Southampton	FlyBe

Other travel information

Rail

Rome – Alessandria	5.28 hours
Rome – Asti	5.49 hours
Rome – Cuneo	7.48 hours
Rome – Novara	5.18 hours
Rome – Vercelli	5.32 hours
Rome – Turin	6.13 hours

Road

Turin is well served by *autostradas*. The A4 heads east to Milan and beyond, the A5 goes north in Valle D'Aosta, France and the Mont Blanc tunnel, the A32 goes west into France via the Freyjus tunnel, the A6 connects to the Adriatic and Genoa and the A21 heads east to Piacenza and the A1.

Rome – Turin	682 kms, 6.45 hours

Puglia

Puglia, in the heel of Italy, has a long coastline facing the Ionian and Adriatic seas. It has a population of 3,918,430. Bari is the capital and the main province. Other provinces are Brindisi, Lecce, Foggia and Taranto. This is a region full of historic towns, Roman and Greek ruins and gorgeous seaside resorts. The university town of Lecce has been described as a 'Florence of the south' and is full of great restaurants, bars and shops.

Brindisi is one of the main ports for travelling to Greece and the whole of Puglia has a Greek or Spanish feel, thanks to the architectural influence of past invaders. Those who venture inland will find rolling countryside covered in vines, olive trees and wild flowers. Puglia enjoys practically year-round sunshine with mild winters. The region is noted for its distinctive *Trulli* houses, stone built, circular, one room houses constructed without cement so that they could easily be dismantled when the tax man came around. Ignored for years, they are now very fashionable to buy and restore. Masserie, fortified farmhouses, are also sought after. *Trulli* are very small but sometimes other rooms can be added; they cost around 100,000 euros upwards after restoration. A habitable masseria will be upwards of 300,000 euros. New-build, two bedroom villas by the sea are approximately 120, 000 euros.

UK travel links

New scheduled direct flights are now in operation to Bari:

Bari	London Stansted	Ryanair
	London Gatwick	BA

Other travel information

Rail

Rome – Bari	4.39 hours
Rome – Brindisi	5.53 hours
Rome – Foggia	4.06 hours
Rome – Lecce	6.22 hours
Rome – Taranto	6.31 hours

Road

The A16 and the A14 connect Puglia with Naples and the north-east. The *autostrada* ends just north of Taranto.

Rome – Bari	460 kms, 4.35 hours
Rome – Lecce	600 kms, 6.15 hours

Sardinia (Sardegna)

The second largest island in the Mediterranean, Sardinia has turquoise seas, marvellous beaches and rugged, mountainous countryside. The island has a population of 1,584,203 and its provinces are Cagliari, Nuoro, Oristano and Sassari. Its economy is based on sheep rearing for wool and cheese – Sardinian pecorino is world famous – but the main industry is tourism. This island has become the favourite holiday destination of Italians who love the dramatic coastline, pretty fishing ports and Sardinian nightlife. Every summer, of course, hundreds of thousands of tourists from other parts of the world descend on Sardinia. Winters are mild but wet – the average minimum temperature is 10–20° C – while from April to October it is very hot. In July and August, the heat is intense and it is best to be somewhere next to the sea. The most famous part of Sardinia is the *Costa Smeralda* (the Emerald Coast), established by the Aga Khan in the 1960s, and now a holiday playground for the very rich. The Italian Prime Minister Silvio Berlusconi has not one, but three houses here, and the luxury boats moored in the marinas are something to see. Leisure activities centre on the island's many beaches but there are also two world-class golf courses here.

There is a vast choice of property for sale in Sardinia. A lot of houses and apartments are in self-contained resorts near the sea but with shared facilities such as bars, restaurants and swimming pools. Examples: one bedroom apartment in a small condominium with living room, open plan kitchen and terrace – 80,000 euros. Typical restored Sardinian house with two bedrooms, two bathrooms, small garden and a few minutes walk from the sea – 290,000 euros. Six bedroom, six bathroom, luxury newbuild villa, 100 metres from the sea, with small garden. 1,500,000 euros.

UK travel links

Meridiana flies direct scheduled flights from London Gatwick to Sardinia, flying twice a week from Gatwick airport to Olbia, nearest airport to the

Costa Smeralda. Ryanair flies twice a day to Alghero. There are charter flights from the UK in the summer. Alitalia and Meridiana fly to Cagliari and Olbia from the Italian mainland, from cities such as Rome, Milan and Bologna (S = Summer only):

Alghero	London Stansted	Ryanair
	Manchester	(S) BA
Cagliari	Luton	Air Volare
	London Gatwick	BA
Olbia	London Gatwick	Meridiana

Other travel information

Ferry

By ferry from Genoa, Livorno, Civitavecchia, Naples and Palermo. Journey times are from 7 to 13 hours.

Road and ferry

Rome – Cagliari   645 kms, 11 hours

Sicily (Sicilia)

Sicily is the biggest island in the Mediterranean, measuring 112 miles from north to south and 170 miles across. The Greeks, Romans, Arabs, Normans, French and Spanish, all of whom ruled over the island at one time, have each left their imprint on the island's architecture, language and customs and Sicily therefore has its own, unique identity and rich history. Mount Etna, rising in the centre of the island, is the highest active volcano in Europe. The islands of Stromboli and Vulcano are also active volcanoes. Sicily has a population of 4,793,417. Palermo is the regional capital and the other provinces are

Agrigento, Caltanissetta, Catania, Enna, Messina, Ragusa, Siracusa and Trapani. Many small islands surround Sicily, including Lampedusa, Pantelleria and Lipari. Sicily has a Mediterranean climate with very hot summers and mild, rainy winters. It is the most densely populated island in the Mediterranean, with a population of over 5 million.

Inland life is hard for those who are not used to it and foreigners usually buy property in the tourist areas – a one bedroom apartment in the popular resort of Taormina will cost 150,000 euros, a one bedroom apartment in Giardini-Naxos will be 100,000 euros and a new-build villa with a swimming pool on the coast, but in one of the less fashionable resorts, will be 400,000 euros. Remember that Sicily is an island: the cost of living is high because so many things have to be imported. That also goes for Sardinia.

Most foreigners want to know if there is a problem with the Mafia in Sicily. I have asked people who have bought properties there and the general opinion is that the organized crime families of years past have largely lost their influence. You will be fine if you want to buy an apartment. If you want to build a big house, however, or buy a Sicilian business it might be best to make friends first with the 'influential people' in your area. The culture of connectedness – being respectful to the right people and the 'I do you a favour, now you owe me a favour' attitude – still exists.

UK travel links

Palermo has two daily flights by Ryanair to Stansted and Catania is served by charter flights from the UK in the summer months (S = Summer only):

Catania	London Gatwick	(S) Charter
	Manchester	(S) BMI, MyTravel, Thomas Cook
Palermo	London Gatwick	(S) Monarch
	London Stansted	Ryanair
	Luton	(S) Monarch

Other travel information

Rail

Rome – Catania	9.05 hours
Rome – Palermo	10.50 hours
Rome – Trapani	14.38 hours

Ferry

There are regular ferry crossings from Villa San Giovanni to Messina.

Road

Rome – Catania   800 kms, 8.15 hours
Rome – Palermo   943 kms, 9.30 hours

Trentino-Alto Adige

This region in the north-east of Italy, which has a population of 959,424, is a land of majestic mountains, castles, glaciers and nature reserves. Trentino and Alto Adige were granted autonomous status after World War II and both retain very different characters, although now joined in a single region. Alto Adige, which is also called South Tirol, is predominantly German speaking while Trentino is Italian speaking. The provinces are Trento and Bolzano-Bozen. The region has an Alpine climate – moderately warm in summer and sunny and cold in winter. This is a fine wine-growing area and is also noted for its apple and pear crops. Property hunters will want to investigate the wonderful ski resorts – Madonna Di Campiglio, Martino di Castrozza, Moena and the Kronplatz ski fields. Property is reasonably priced but this region is not particularly popular with foreign buyers.

UK travel links

The nearest airport to the Trentino Alto-Adige area is Verona, with daily flights from Stansted by Ryanair and from Gatwick by British Airways (S = Summer only):

Verona	Bristol	(S) Charter
	Leeds/Bradford	(S) Charter
	London Gatwick	BA
	London Stansted	Ryanair
	Manchester	(S) BA, Britannia, Excel

Other travel information

Rail

Rome – Bolzano	5.59 hours
Rome – Trento	5.25 hours

Road

The A22 *autostrada* dissects the region, running north to Austria and south to Verona and beyond.

Rome – Bolzano	650 kms, 6.30 hours
Rome – Trento	600 kms, 5.55 hours

Tuscany (Toscana)

When most people dream of buying a property in Italy they think of Tuscany with its stunning landscapes, perfect medieval towns, and museums and galleries crammed with artistic treasures. The food and wines aren't bad either. This region, which has a population of 3,447,067, and whose provinces are Arezzo, Florence, Grosseto, Livorno, Lucca, Massa-Carrara, Pisa, Pistoia, Prato and Siena is the most popular destination for tourists. Property hunters in the most fashionable parts of this region, however, need to have large wallets. Some estate agents in the sought-after Chianti area will not deign to deal with you unless you have 700,000 euros to spend. A three bedroom apartment in Florence will be over a million euros. But there still some good deals to be had if you are prepared to hunt around. In the north of Tuscany you can buy a village house to restore for 80,000 euros. A stone farmhouse to restore is 60,000 euros upwards, depending on the area it is in and the quality of its views.

UK travel links

Meridiana/Alitalia has direct daily flights to Florence from London Gatwick. British Airways from Gatwick and Ryanair from Stansted have direct daily flights to Pisa airport. There are also daily flights from Birmingham to Pisa with MyTravel, and BMI Baby fly from East Midlands. British Airways has flights from Manchester to Pisa (S = Summer only):

Florence	London Gatwick	Meridiana/Alitalia
Pisa	Birmingham	MyTravel
	Bristol	(S) Charter
	East Midlands	BMI Baby
	Leeds/Bradford	(S) Charter
	London Stansted	Ryanair
	London Gatwick	BA, (S) Air 2000, Monarch
	Manchester	BA, (S) Britannia, Air 2000

Other travel information

Rail

Eurostar from London Waterloo via Paris to Florence.

Rome – Arezzo	1.25 hours
Rome – Grosseto	1.33 hours
Rome – Florence	1.35 hours
Rome – Livorno	2.47 hours
Rome – Lucca	3.20 hours
Rome – Pisa	2.57 hours
Rome – Siena	3.08 hours

Road

The A1 runs the length and breadth of Tuscany and the region has an excellent roads system.

Rome – Florence	285 kms, 3.10 hours
Rome – Pisa	380 kms, 3.55 hours
Rome – Lucca	355 kms, 3.40 hours

Umbria

I have to declare an interest here since this is the region of Italy where I have chosen to live. Halfway between Florence and Rome, land-locked Umbria describes itself as the green heart of Italy and the landscape is just as beautiful as neighbouring Tuscany although a little more wild and uncultivated. Umbria has a population of 834,133, and its provinces are Perugia and Terni. It is mountainous and hilly, is crossed by the Apennines, and has Lake Trasimeno within its borders. Perugia is the regional capital and other important cities are Assisi, Spoleto, Orvieto, Todi and Gubbio. Agriculture and tourism are the main sources of employment and the climate is warm and humid in summer and wet and quite cold in winter. The quality of light and the mists that descend on Umbria during autumn and winter, however, make it a magical place.

Property prices in Umbria have risen sharply in the last few years but with careful searching, there are still good deals to be found. An apartment to restore in one of the medieval villages will be upwards of 70,000 euros, a stone farmhouse to restore will be approximately 250,000 euros, and expect to pay 400,000 upwards for a restored property, depending on area, the amount of land and views.

UK travel links

British Airways and Alitalia have daily flights to Rome's Fiumicino airport. Ryanair and easyJet fly into Rome's Ciampino airport. From both airports it is a drive through Lazio into Umbria. Travellers from the UK can also fly to Pisa or Florence and drive (S = Summer only):

Rome (Fiumicino)	Birmingham	BA
	Cork	Aer Lingus
	Dublin	Alitalia
	Edinburgh	(S) BA
	London Gatwick	BA, Alitalia

	London Heathrow	BA, Alitalia
	Manchester	BA
Rome (Ciampino)	London Stansted	Ryanair, easyJet
	Edinburgh	(S) FlyGlobespan
	Glasgow	(S) FlyGlobespan

Other travel information

Rail

Rome – Orvieto	0.52 hours
Rome – Perugia	2.12 hours
Rome – Terni	0.49 hours

Road

There is an excellent road network with the A1 running north to south.

Rome – Perugia	180 kms, 2.30 hours

Valle D'Aosta

Admired for its Alpine scenery, fortified castles and renowned ski resorts, Valle D'Aosta is in the north-west corner of Italy and is the most mountainous region of Italy. Entirely surrounded by the Alps – Monte Bianco, the Matterhorn, Monte Rosa and Gran Paradiso – it is a paradise for winter and summer sports enthusiasts. There are glaciers, alpine lakes and forests teeming with wildlife. It has a population of 1,201,173. Aosta is the capital of the region, where both Italian and French are the officially recognized languages. Another important town is St Vincent, which has its own casino. The famous ski resorts of Courmayeur and Cervinia are here as well as the fortified castles of Fenis, Issogne and Aymavilles. Valle D'Aosta has an Alpine climate – warm but not too hot in summer and temperatures are very low, often below freezing, but sunny in winter.

Tourism is the major industry with visitors coming all year round, but agriculture and raising sheep and cattle are also a major part of the local economy.

The authorities in Valle D'Aosta have restricted the amount of new construction in the region in an attempt to preserve the natural beauty of the area, but there is still a good mix of property for sale. Traditional Valdostana wood and stone chalets are scarce now but if you can find one it will cost approximately 140,000 euros plus restoration costs. A newly built, one bedroom apartment in a major ski resort such as Cervinia will cost approximately 150,000 euros. New four bedroom villas with gardens and panoramic views are on sale for an average 400,000 euros.

UK travel links

It is not possible to fly direct from the UK to Valle D'Aosta but nearby airports are Milan and Turin (S = Summer only):

Milan Bergamo	Cardiff	BMI Baby
	London Stansted	Ryanair
Milan Linate	London Heathrow	BA, BMI, Alitalia
	London Gatwick	easyJet
	London Stansted	easyJet
Milan Malpensa	Birmingham	BA, FlyBe
	Cork	Aer Lingus
	Dublin	Aer Lingus, Alitalia
	East Midlands	BMI Baby
	Leeds/Bradford	Channel Express
	London Heathrow	BA, Alitalia
	Manchester	(S) BA, Charter
	Southampton	FlyBe
Turin	London Gatwick	(S) Air 2000
	London Stansted	Ryanair
	Manchester	(S) Air 2000

Other travel information

Rail

Rome – Aosta   7.56 hours

Road

Rome – Aosta   755 kms, 7.20 hours

Veneto

This region of Italy has some of the most majestic peaks of the Dolomites, with numerous ski resorts including chic Cortina D'Ampezzo, but it is Venice that everyone falls for. Uniquely beautiful with its canals, bridges and outstanding architecture, it is considered the most romantic city in the world. Veneto has a population of 4,540,026 and its provinces are Venice – the regional capital – and other important cities are Verona, Padova, Vicenza, Treviso, Rovigo and Belluno. Veneto has two climates – maritime in the lagoon zone, which means hot and humid summers and fog and rain in winter – and Alpine in the north. Tourism is the main industry. Veneto's other towns and cities are a delight as well: Verona, best known for its Romeo and Juliet setting, Padua with its Giotto frescoes and Treviso with its little canals and home of the Benetton business. Take a deep gulp if you are contemplating buying property in Venice. A small one bedroom apartment in a restored palazzo on the Grand Canal will cost 1.5 million euros; however, a two bedroom apartment close to Rialto is a more affordable 400,000 euros. In Treviso you can find a two bedroom apartment for 160,000 euros.

UK travel links

British Airways fly to Marco Polo airport. Ryanair flies to Treviso airport, 18 miles inland. BMIBaby flies from Birmingham to Marco Polo. easyJet flies from Bristol to Marco Polo and also flies a weekly service from East Midland airport. British Airways has a daily service from Manchester to Marco Polo (S = Summer only):

Venice (Marco Polo)	Bristol	easyJet, (S) Charter
	Birmingham	BA, BMI Baby, (S) Monarch
	Dublin	Aer Lingus
	East Midlands	easyJet
	London Gatwick	BA, (S) Monarch
	London Heathrow	BMI
	London Stansted	easyJet, Ryanair
	Manchester	BA, (S) Britannia, Astraeus, Monarch, MyTravel
Venice (Treviso)	London Stansted	Ryanair

Other travel information

Rail

Venice has excellent train links to all of Europe, including the famous Venice-Simplon Orient Express.

Rome – Belluno	6.26 hours
Rome – Padua	4.00 hours
Rome – Rovigo	3.34 hours
Rome – Treviso	4.56 hours
Rome – Venice	4.32 hours
Rome – Verona	4.20 hours

Road

Rome – Venice	540 kms, 5.35 hours
Rome – Treviso	560 kms, 5.40 hours

3 Renting a home in Italy

Research has shown that the single biggest mistake people make when buying a property in Italy is choosing to live in the wrong area. Perhaps they have been on holiday in a particular part of the country, fallen in love with the place while the sun is shining, and not considered what it would be like to live there in winter when everything closes down and the countryside looks grim. Other people, who cannot afford to buy a property in picture-postcard-perfect Chiantishire, settle for a cheaper house in a less attractive part of Tuscany and then find *la dolce vita* does not live up to their dreams. The solution is to rent first to make sure you are really doing the right thing. Remember that buying and selling a property in Italy is expensive so if you are not completely happy with the house that you buy you may lose money by having to re-sell it. Renting is prudent because it is easily reversible. You can experience life in a particular part of Italy and then move on if it is not for you.

Examples of why you should rent first

We were saved from buying an unsuitable property because we had the chance to live in it and explore the area. This converted farmhouse – in the Lazio region – was being rented to tourists while it was on the market so we decided to stay there over a July weekend and see how we liked it. On the first night of our stay we went out for a pizza, returned at about 11pm and were greeted by one of the most incredible sights we have ever seen. The land all around the house was lit up by thousands and thousands of fireflies. It looked as if fairies had invaded the garden and we were utterly entranced, sitting up until 2am drinking wine and just watching this magical show of nature. My husband declared that that was it, we were *definitely* buying the house. But the next day, reality intervened and I was not so sure. Now that I had time to look at the property closely, without the owner and estate agent being around, I saw that it had been poorly restored and the layout was strange. To get to some of the bedrooms you had to go through other bedrooms, plus the windows were very high up – when you sat down you couldn't see out of them. The faint hum of traffic from the valley below was a niggle but the final nail in the coffin was when we discovered the nearest village had only a couple of rather grubby bars. I wanted interesting shops, restaurants and markets on our doorstep and cafes where we could sit and watch the world go by. That night we witnessed the same incredible light show in the garden and had, ahem, a heated discussion about whether or not to buy the house. The firefly season only lasts for about six weeks and it was not a good enough reason to buy a property that clearly had flaws. In the end, we both agreed that the house and the area were not right for us. Those few days of staying in the property and in that particular area – experiencing what it would really be like to live there – made up our minds. Although we have never seen as many fireflies again, we know we did the right thing in not buying the house.

When we bought the farmhouse that we live in now, we came out one weekend with some close friends to show them the property. We booked into a local bed and breakfast, run by an expatriate. We arrived at about 11pm and it was obvious that our hostess had been at the gin because the bottle was well down and she was rather unsteady on her feet and quite aggressive in her demeanour. We joined her rather reluctantly for a nightcap and she asked if we were here on holiday. 'We've just bought a house not very far away from here,' I said proudly. 'Oh, for God's sake, how pathetic!' she exclaimed and then went into a rant about how she hated Italy, hated Italians, wished she had never come to live here and what fools we were for buying a house and falling for all this 'Italian peasant crap'. We were taken aback – so much for our Italian dream – and our friends' faces were a picture as they tried not to laugh. We have since discovered that this woman is infamous locally for her tirades against the Italian way of life. She obviously should have rented first! As I have said already, there is a big difference between a holiday in Italy and the day-to-day reality of actually living here. If this woman had rented a house first, she might have discovered that this life was not for her and she wouldn't be stuck in a B and B, terrorizing her guests. And no, I don't recommend her establishment to tourists.

Short-term rentals

Finding a short-term holiday rental that will let you have a good look around a specific part of Italy is a very good idea. You can rent a house or apartment through a holiday lettings agency or a travel company, or you can make your own way to the area and find accommodation on your own initiative. It is relatively easy to find houses to rent – apart from July and in the month of August when most of Italy is on holiday. Landlords are only too willing to rent out their properties in winter as well. To find a holiday rental apartment in the *centro storico* of an Italian town, walk through the neighbourhood looking for *affitasi* (for rent) signs or go to an *agente immobiliare*. Most rents will be negotiable and you should try to get a discount if you are staying for a week or more. If you have found a house that you are interested in buying, and it is habitable, there is no harm in asking if it would be possible to stay there. You might have to arrange this and then return a week or so later, as we did, but just being there for one or two nights might be enough to make your mind up.

Long-term rentals

If you want a long-term rental, your best bet is to try to find accommodation through personal contacts or to use a professional lettings agency. If you want to rent in a big city such as Florence, Rome or Milan you can search the apartment listings in local newspapers or expatriate publications. You have to be quick off the mark though because good, reasonably priced accommodation is always in short supply in the big cities.

The Italian government has instituted very strict laws to protect the rights of people who rent property. The most common contract is called a *contratto libero* that is nicknamed the ' four plus four'. The law states a landlord has to guarantee rental of the property for four years, after which it will automatically be renewed for another four years unless the landlord gives written notice six months before the first expiry date – ie after three and a half years. He has to have good reason for wanting the property back – he wants to live in it himself, or a close family member wants to live there, or he wants to sell the property. Some

Italian landlords try to get round this automatic renewal clause – they say their daughter or son is getting married and they need the property back, for example, but it is usually because they want to get a new tenant so they can raise the rent. If landlords force you to leave on a premise such as this and you find out later that it is not true, you theoretically have recourse and the landlord may be forced to pay one to three years' rent as compensation.

Because of the conditions attached to the *contratto libero* landlords are very particular about the kind of tenants they will accept. Basically, once a tenant takes possession he can stay there for up to eight years, so if you are very keen on a particular property, put your best foot forward and do what you can to impress the landlord.

Disdetta

As a tenant you are permitted to get out of the four-year rental cycle by giving six months written notice (*disdetta*) at any time. However, you must give good reason (*motivi gravi*) for doing so – losing your job, moving abroad, etc. If you do want to terminate your rental contract send a letter by registered mail with a return receipt – available at the post office, it is called a *raccomandata con ricevuto di ritorno* – so that you can be absolutely sure your landlord has received it. You can negotiate a three months' notice period with your landlord, and in some cases, only a one-year rental contract, but this must be agreed between both parties and written down in the rental contract.

Rent and deposit for damages

When you sign the contract you will be asked to pay six months' rent (*l'affitto*). Half of that sum is held as a *cauzione* against damage and will be returned, plus interest, when you leave. The rest is advance rent. Rent will thereafter be paid quarterly. You will have to pay to register the contract at your local *ufficio del registro* if the rental is above 1,200 euros a month – you and the owner will split the fee, which is normally 2 per cent of the first year's rental.

Unfurnished and furnished accommodation

Unfurnished property in Italy is completely unfurnished – your house or apartment may not even have a kitchen, carpets or curtains. Friends in Milan, who moved to the city for work, were astonished to find the previous tenants had taken the kitchen with them. When they queried this with the letting agency they were told: 'You wouldn't want someone else's kitchen anyway, would you? You will want to put in your own.' My friends, faced with an apartment stripped to the bare bones, discovered that the previous tenants had even considered taking up the parquet flooring that they had laid but realized they couldn't do so without ruining it. If you are taking over from an outgoing tenant it will save you time and money to buy all his furniture and appliances, so keep this in mind when viewing rental apartments. Note that furnished accommodation in Italy is available and does not usually include bed linen, towels and kitchen equipment such as cutlery and saucepans.

Condominiums

If you are renting an apartment in a large building ask if the condominium fee (*spese*) – general expenses for running the building – is included in the monthly rental. These are the costs for heating, cleaning, elevator maintenance, *portinaio* service and rubbish collection. Check with the *amministratore di condominio* (administrator of the building) that the previous tenant has paid off his rent and outstanding *spese* because you could become liable for someone else's back payments. Enquire about rules regarding children or pets, if you have them.

Tenants' responsibilities

A tenant is usually expected to clean and paint the property at his expense before he moves out. He may also be liable for any repairs inside the house during the duration of his tenancy. The landlord will pay for works outside the house, such as repairs to the roof, chimney, guttering, stairs, windows and shutters and he should be – but is not always – responsible for plumbing and heating repairs. Establish who is responsible for the different repairs and get it written on your rental contract. All utilities – electricity, gas and telephone – will be the responsibility of the tenant. Landlords are permitted to raise the rent by a small increment every year in keeping with the Italian government's cost of living index.

Commission

You will have to pay the *agente immobilare* or renting agency a commission for finding the property. This fee varies, depending on where you are in Italy. In Rome, for example, it is one month's rent or 8 per cent. In Milan it is 10 to 18 per cent. In smaller towns it will be 10 per cent. Again, you may be able to negotiate a discount.

Cost of rental

At the time of writing the Italian rental market is very active. Rome rentals are as expensive as Paris, London and New York – one agent told me that prices have doubled in the last three years. Unless your company is footing the bill, you will pay a small fortune to live right in the centre of one of the big cities. A *monocamera* – an apartment with living room and bedroom ajoined – costs 2,000 euros a month in central Rome. Go slightly further out into the suburbs and you will find much better value with a one bedroom rental for 1,200 euros a month. A three bedroom family apartment in Rome will cost from 2,500 euros to 10,000. In Milan you can find a one bedroom apartment for 1,500 euros a month and a family property for 2,500 euros upwards. Prices in the countryside will obviously be a lot lower. Remember, however, that most people want an extra bedroom so that they can have guests to stay, so you will have to look for a larger than normal property.

Leaving

When it is time to leave your rental property, you will need to write to confirm this. Here is an example of a suitable letter:

---

address
date

Dear...
Gentile...

I am the tenant of the appartment/house at...
*Sono l'affitturario/a dell' appartamento/casa
sito in...*

With this letter please accept notice that I will
be leaving the apartment on...
*Con la presente le dó notizia che dalla data...
làscero il suddetto appartamento.*

I will be grateful if you would return the
deposit of...
Prego, vogliate restiturirmi la cauzione di...

Thank you for your assistance.
Ringraziandovi per la vostra assistenza.

---

4 Searching for a house

When you have done your preliminary research into the type of house that you want and that you can afford, you can book flights and make appointments with estate agents *(agente immobiliare)*. Do not think you can simply turn up in some seaside resort or medieval *borgo* in the hope that you will discover your dream house. By and large, Italian properties do not have 'for sale' signs outside their doors and you need an estate agent to show you what is currently on the market. By e-mail or telephone, inform an estate agent of the dates you are coming out, tell them your budget and your wish list and ask to be shown suitable properties. When you get to your chosen area, you will be able to look in estate agency windows – but they may be busy and unable to show you properties in the time that you have available. That is why you should plan ahead.

Estate agents

Most Italian agents have a working knowledge of English so you are unlikely at this stage to need a translator. There are also many English estate agents working in Italy. Check that the estate agent is a member of FIAIP (*Federazione Italiana Agenti Immobiliari Professionali*) and is registered with the local chamber of commerce (*camera di commercio*). Agents should also have prominently displayed at their office and on business cards their *Partita* IVA (VAT tax number). All of this denotes that an agent has passed professional exams and is well versed in Italian property law. It also signals that he or she is an established estate agent and therefore probably accustomed to dealing with foreign buyers. Estate agents do not have exclusives on properties so verify that you are not being taken to see the same house by different agents. Be very firm about what you don't want – for example, you may not want to be attached to another property and you certainly don't want to have an electricity pylon right outside your front door. Get the estate agent to weed out these kinds of properties – showing them to you is just a waste of time for everyone.

Contacting an estate agent

If you want to e-mail an estate agent to get some information on available properties, here is an example of what to write:

I have been looking at your Web site.
Ho visitato il vostro sito web.

I would like to buy a house in your area, preferably not far from...
Vorrei acquistare una casa nella vostra zona, preferibilmente non lontano da...

I am looking for a house with... bedrooms, to restore, and with a small amount of land.
Sto cercando una casa con... camere da letto, da ristrutturare, con un po' di terreno.

My budget is approximately...
Io vorrei spendere intorno...

Can you let me know if you have any suitable properties?
Gradirei sapere se avete qualcosa da proporre?

I will be in your area... and would like to make an appointment with you, if you are available.
Io dovrei venire a... e gradirei un appuntamento con lei se lei e(accent) disponibile.

Thank you very much.
Ringraziandovi.

Take notes

When you view properties have a notebook and pen handy – you will be surprised how each house you see seems to merge into the next. By the end of a long day when you have seen four or five houses you can be quite confused, so it is important to jot down your initial impressions of each house in order to review them later. Write down the good and the bad points about each property. If you want, take a video camera or just an ordinary camera as another *aide-memoire*. Make sure you have a compass. This will enable you to check which direction each property faces – you need to do this to see how much sun the house and the garden get and whether it will be possible to see sunsets at night.

Rough ground

Remember to dress properly. You will, in all likelihood, have to walk through fields to isolated properties or tramp around derelict buildings, so you need proper shoes like boots or trainers – not flip-flops or sandals. These will also help protect you from snakes. Wear trousers or long skirts to protect your legs from nettles and other spiky plants so you can freely explore the terrain surrounding the properties.

Mobile phones

It may be important for you for work purposes to have mobile telephone reception at your house – take your mobile phone with you and check the signal.

Perseverance

Searching for a property is not a holiday, so do not be sidetracked by long, boozy lunches or detours to local art galleries and museums. These visits to Italy – with flights, accommodation and car hire – will cost money that you will not be able to recoup, but this money will not be wasted. Regard it as the beginning of your investment. Do not isolate yourself in some big, tourist hotel. Stay in local *agriturismos* or small, family-run hotels. It is much more fun, it gives you a better understanding of the area you are exploring and you will be able to ask lots of questions. You may find after a decent immersion in one part of Italy that the area is not suitable for you. What we did during our house hunting was to devote ourselves entirely to the task in hand every day – sometimes foregoing lunch to travel long distances – but then reward ourselves with a fabulous dinner in the evenings.

Maximize your chances

When dealing with estate agents in Italy, remember that they are inundated with people from all over the world, all looking for the same dream house as you. They see all kinds of time-wasters – so-called 'property tourists' who enjoy looking around Italian houses but are not seriously interested in buying. They also see people with completely unrealistic ideas about the kind of house they can get for their money. They want a farmhouse in Tuscany, an olive grove and five hectares of vines, for 200,000 euros, for example. Estate agents also have to deal with people who keep changing their minds about what they want – one day it's a small house on the edge of a town, the next day it's a ruined convent with 15 bedrooms. You will impress estate agents – and they will allocate you more time and tip you off about new properties yet to come onto the market – if you show that you have put some thought into the kind of property that you want and that you are not fooling around with your time or theirs. You have to make estate agents work for you. This is a competitive market, so get them on your side.

Check things out

Of course you must remain on your guard with estate agents. As in all professions, there are good and bad ones. To them this is just a job and they want to off-load properties as quickly as possible, especially the troublesome ones that have been on the market for a long time. Do not take their word on anything – verify everything to your own satisfaction. Estate agents will insist, for example, that the property is sunny all day when the reality is that you lose the sun behind a hill in the late afternoon – this is where the compass will come in handy and why you must come back at different times of the day if you are really interested in buying. Estate agents might tell you that there will be no problem finding water on the property – but can they guarantee that? They may underplay the problems of rights of way and *strada vicinale* (communal roads) so be wary if there appears to be a well-worn path through the property. Some estate agents buy the properties themselves and sell them on at inflated prices – there is nothing illegal in this – but you should be aware of this practice because they will not tell you. Make sure you meet the owners if at all possible, or be certain that the asking price the agent has quoted you is reasonable.

Architectural features

If you are going for a complete ruin, try to find a house with some original architectural features like stone arches, vaulted ceilings, old terracotta floors and lovely stonework. Does the property have other buildings – a barn that could be converted into further accommodation, a wood-burning pizza oven, a cantina where you can store wine? Does the land on which the house stands support an outdoor life – it needs to be wide enough to have at least one outdoor eating area, so beware of terraced land that falls away steeply – and check that there is a suitable piece of flat land not too far away from the house for a swimming pool. Consider the height of the land on which a house stands. If a house is built in a valley you are more likely to be troubled by mosquitoes, heat in summer and damp in winter. If it is on a hillside (although not too high up) you will get cooling breezes that could be a lifesaver in summer and you will be less troubled by insects.

Views

The view from your property will be important – you want an outlook that is typically Italian, whether it's a view of rooftops, or a valley dotted with cypress trees. Reject houses if they have motorways, factories or reprocessing plants within view – Italians are very bad at landscaping and these will always be eyesores, not to mention the problems you could have with bad odours and poor air quality.

Walk the boundaries

The estate agent should bring a map that shows the house and its land clearly marked. If you are seriously interested in the property, walk all around the boundaries so you can see what you are buying. Check who owns the next field, how near you are to other buildings, ask about rights of way for local people (*diritti di passaggi)* and *strada vicinale.*

Water and other services

Check that there is water on site – either from a mains source or a well. Watch the French film *Jean de Florette* to see what a nightmare lack of water can be. Confirm that there is already an electricity and a gas supply or that it will not be too expensive to bring these utilities to the house. Think carefully about the access road – if it is a dirt track it may be difficult to negotiate in winter weather.

Live/work space

Establish that the house in question is entirely liveable space – some houses in the Italian countryside are designated part live/work space and you will not be allowed to live in the work space. A friend of mine was very excited when she was shown a wreck of a house in Tuscany. The building measured 150 sq metres and it had wonderful views. She was about to put in an offer when the *geometra* (more about his role later) checked the records at the commune and discovered only 55 sq metres was officially liveable space. The rest of the building had been put up without permission. There is a system based on the *condono* – a kind of amnesty that the Italian government grants every now and then for unapproved buildings – but you must not, under any circumstances, depend on this. There are no guarantees that you would get a successful *condono* and you should not buy a live/work property on this basis unless you really are going to live and work there. My friend regretfully pulled out of the deal.

Property already converted

Buying an old stone farmhouse to convert is most people's ideal, but do not discount a house that is already habitable. Be careful, however, that you are not purchasing someone else's problems or inadequate restoration. People in Italy do some or all of the restoration work themselves, with very mixed standards of quality. Have the property checked out by a surveyor. Is the basic structure – the roof and walls – well restored? Is there any sign of damp or subsidence? Is the general layout roughly as you want it or easily convertible to your tastes? If you are in a known earthquake zone, has the house been built or restored to earthquake standards? Did the previous owner have planning permission for everything that was done – you do not want to buy the house and then be forced to pull down the lot. Check that there are enough power points and that the wiring is sound. Get someone to give the central heating a proper check. Have they put in cheap tiles instead of lovely, handmade terracotta ones? Do not assume that because the property does not have a swimming pool, it is because the owner didn't want one. Confirm that you can get permission.

Planning decisions

If you are buying a property in a town, check whether it is in an area that is going to be developed. You can go to the local town hall to do this. If you are in the country and can afford to buy land around you, do so, even if it is zoned as being rural. Planning decisions can change over the years and you do not want to find yourself hedged in by a housing estate in 20 years' time or have some farmer build an ugly agricultural *rimessa* within your line of vision.

Part ownership

Ask for proof that the person who has put the house up for sale owns it in its entirety. Because of Italian inheritance laws, brothers, sisters and parents can be entitled to a share in a sibling's estate, so it is quite common for a house to be owned by many members of one family. You will need to verify that everyone has given permission to sell. One person can hold up the sale of a house even though the rest of the family want to sell, and it is better not to get involved in situations like this because the arguments can rumble on for years. Unless you are buying a large estate, steer clear of properties with tenants in situ elsewhere on the property.

Keep checking

Do not be afraid to ask the estate agent lots of questions about a house you are interested in. Go back several times, at different times of the day and night, to see how quiet or noisy it is. If possible, see it in different weather – most places look delightful on a sunny day but you need to know how it looks on a grey, rainy day. Keep asking yourself if there is something you have overlooked. If you can, visit your prospective neighbours and see how they react to the idea of you moving in – you will be able to judge if they are going to be amenable and helpful even if you cannot understand what they are saying.

If you are buying in a town, city or coastal resort, check what is around you, Will you have to put up with a camping ground for German nudists or an influx of 18–30 holidaymakers? What is the place like in the off-season? Is there an infrastructure all year round or does the resort close down for winter and become bleak and unfriendly?

Adventures in house buying

You will be surprised at the sheer physical toll of house hunting in Italy and how many hours it takes to view properties. Houses are scattered around the countryside and you will find yourself travelling for many hours in a day. In my own case, I saw about 40 properties before settling on the one that we bought. Be prepared for setbacks and strange situations. We fell in love with one farmhouse in Tuscany, agreed to pay the asking price to ensure there was no danger of losing it to another buyer and left the matter in the hands of a British estate agent, resident in Italy. We flew back triumphantly to London, sketching renovation plans on British Airways napkins, and heard – nothing. Whenever I called the agent for a progress report he told me he was having trouble contacting the owner, a very rich woman who lived in Rome. For four weeks he fobbed me off until I began to smell a rat. We had a row on the telephone. I stopped calling and he never phoned me back. I assume the owner took the house off the market or someone else bought the property for more than the asking price. It was a bitter blow because to our minds the house was already ours and it nearly put us off the whole idea of buying a house in Italy. But we put it down to experience and restarted the search.

On another occasion, we were invited to a tea party on a wet Sunday afternoon by a British couple working as estate agents and renovators. Apparently this was a regular social occasion where clients who had bought properties or were in the process of buying properties from this couple could meet and swap stories. They were all perfectly nice people but rather smug about the bargain ruins they had purchased and patronizing about the Italian way of life. After tea we were taken to see properties on a hillside. 'That house is owned by a couple from Harrogate, that house is owned by a couple from Scotland, that house is owned by a couple of Danes and that house is owned by a couple from London,' the agent said. There were two or three houses on the hillside left for sale and apparently he thought we would want live in this strange expatriate community, with not an Italian in sight. We thanked them for the tea and sandwiches and left.

Another time we were taken to see a house in the beautiful area of Val D'Orcia in Tuscany – where 'The English Patient' was filmed – and found that the asking price for a ruin next to a 40-metre pylon bristling with electricity was half a million pounds. Apparently the value of the housing stock in the Val D'Orcia has soared because the immensely rich Bulgari brothers have bought properties there – one has put in an underground car park for 30 cars. Farmers who still own properties in this stunning valley now believe the world is full of millionaires and have hiked up the prices to ridiculous levels.

We were taken by an Italian agent one day to see a beautiful, ruined old house, with a private chapel on a hillside. The property had been on the market for several years and the agent admitted it was over-priced by 20 or 30 per cent. The owner, he said, was an uneducated peasant farmer who had simply plucked a figure out of his head as the price at which he would sell the house. However, when any interested party tried to make a negotiated offer, the farmer would not only turn it down and say he was mortally offended, he would raise the price even further. The reason was that this farmer had no need of the money – he was already living on a nice piece of land with his chickens and his cows – and to him, this was just a game. He liked the idea of having a house that other people wanted, he liked being regarded as a man of property, he liked having foreigners come and plead with him to sell. The estate agent said it was highly unlikely the house would ever be sold until the old man died – but he thought he should keep showing the property just in case.

You will discover that some property owners still live in the house that is for sale and it is charming at first to be offered home-made wine or newly distilled *grappa* by eager vendors. The novelty soon wears off. I lost count of the number of times we had to drink foul beverages in living rooms decorated with crucifixes or pictures of the Madonna, when what we really wanted to do was get the hell out of there and have a cold beer in a cafe. One of the properties that we rejected was a weekend house in Tuscany owned by an elderly film director from Rome. He had renovated it in the 1960s and obliterated all the character of the house. There was a monstrous marble and pine bathroom with a sauna and a bath big enough for four – I imagine a few starlets frolicked in there. We knew immediately that it wasn't the house for us but this man had taken the trouble to drive a long distance to meet us and so we had to go through the pretence of looking at the whole property, pretending it was beautiful and drinking his poisonous home-made *grappa*. We thought it was easiest to say that the house was too expensive for us. Big mistake. The old man said he had the perfect plan. We could buy the main house for a reduced price, he would remain in the adjoining guest house, and we would have wonderful parties together all summer! That taught us another lesson – don't pretend a house is too expensive, just say that it is not suitable for your purposes. You don't need to explain yourselves further than this. We were naive in the beginning, wanting to be pleasant and not offend anyone, but we soon toughened up. If you can, respectfully decline the hospitality of the vendors because it slows down the search process and makes it harder to say no, you are not interested in buying that person's house. To make the most of your Italian house-hunting trips, you need to stay focused. Viewing property is not a social occasion and it is better for all concerned if you remain a little remote. Be respectful, but firm and businesslike.

Unless you are very lucky and spy your ideal property immediately, you will have to go through several of these house-hunting trips. Don't be downhearted if your ideal house seems nowhere to be found. Anyone who has already bought a property in Italy will tell you of dispiriting episodes when they were shown a beautiful photograph of a house, drove through rolling hills and picturesque vineyards to see it, trudged through an olive grove full of ancient, gnarled trees, thought euphorically 'this is it, this is my dream home' – only to be disappointed when the house in question turns out to be a stinker. These disappointments are a necessary part of the process – the equivalent of having to kiss a lot of frogs before you find your prince/princess. You need to see what is out there and what kind of value you are getting for your money before you are able to refine your ideas. In all probability, the type of house that you envisaged when you first thought of buying a property in Italy will not be the same as the one that you finally choose. Indeed, you have to keep the balance between fulfilling your wish list and being open to changing some of your ideas in order to find the right property.

Stay focused

Don't waste time seeing properties that you cannot afford. Keep your budget in mind and do not get carried away. I met a woman in an Italian language class who produced photographs of the 'house' she and her husband had bought in Umbria and which she was now trying to re-sell. It was a huge monastery and farm complex, completely unsuitable for a young couple in their thirties. They had been beguiled by the amount of building they were getting for such a low purchase price – but they had not realized that it would cost such a lot to restore. In the cold light of day, they had realized they had made a mistake. We weren't quite as bad as this, but I agreed to view houses that I knew were beyond our budget – because I couldn't resist seeing what they were like. Instead of concentrating on the task in hand, I was daydreaming. I got out of this bad habit quite quickly – it's dispiriting to look at properties you will never be able to afford.

Make up your mind

Be aware too, of a condition called 'indecision syndrome' that can set in. This strikes when you become confused by the wide range of vastly different properties in Italy and are uncertain how to spend your budget. Should you, for instance, spend a small amount of your money on a ruin and the larger amount on restoration? Should you spend the whole of your budget on a really magnificent ruin and hope that you can cobble together enough cash to renovate it over the years? Should you buy into a brand-new development? Do you go for a nicer house, but with less land than you hoped to have? And what happens if you want one house but your partner wants another? It is very easy for house hunters in Italy to become mired in indecision and to keep saying no – always hoping that the next property they view will be absolutely perfect. Some people spend years looking for a property in Italy – losing good ones in the process – because they just cannot make up their minds. I know of one woman who saw 200 houses over two years before finally making up her mind to buy a house in Marche – it has to be a record. Unless you are very rich, you will have to make some compromises because the perfect house is not out there. When you have done enough research – seen many and varied properties – you will know instinctively which property is right for you.

Negotiate

When you are putting in an offer, don't rush in with the asking price, try to negotiate. Vendors in Italy, particularly in popular areas, tend to ask for prices in excess of what a property is worth in the hope that some crazy foreigner who knows no better will come along. Compare the price to similar properties and check how long the property has been on the market (make sure there are no sinister reasons for the house not being snapped up before). If the property has been for sale for some time, there will generally be movement on the price. It's up to you to decide what offer to put in, but you should be able to get some guidance from the estate agent as to what sum the vendor will accept. Always be prepared to walk away if you think the price is unfair.

Final advice

Here is a last tip that was given to me by an American friend. It has proved very useful. Once you have bought your Italian house, stop looking. Don't torture yourself with what might have been. There will always be houses with better views, more interesting architectural features and in better locations. A strange kind of competition surfaces among buyers of Italian houses. I have been to dinner parties in London where several of the guests also owned Italian houses and we were all trying to figure out who got the best bargain. You will always come across someone who bought their house 10 or 20 years ago for a pittance while you have had to fork out considerably more. Be happy with what you end up with.

5 The purchase process

Buying a house in Italy is actually quite safe. Thousands of foreigners have successfully done it so there is no reason why your own purchase should not go through smoothly. The purchase process is nerve-wracking because it takes two to three months and the rules appear complicated to foreign buyers, due to all the bureaucratic procedures involved and the unfamiliarity of the legal system. The key is to acquaint yourself fully with the different stages of buying a house so that you do not feel at the mercy of all the other parties involved.

Legal advice or not

You may wish to employ someone to guide you through the house-buying process in Italy. If you choose to take this route, you will need to decide whether you would prefer to have the services of a bilingual lawyer or whether you will go with a less qualified adviser. There are many lawyers in Italy – and some in the UK – who specialize in helping foreigners buy property. There are also expatriates already resident in Italy who will offer their services as hand-holders for someone who wants to purchase a house. These people are not legally qualified but they will be cheaper than a lawyer and will have a wealth of useful experience. They have been through the process themselves. Alternatively, you can leave the whole process in the hands of your estate agent.

We decided not to go down the path of employing a lawyer. We dealt only with our estate agent and fortunately did not run into any insurmountable problems. I know one person who lost a purchase because, having appointed a bilingual Italian lawyer, became paralyzed by all the potential difficulties that this person uncovered. Having said that, I know that many people would be *appalled* at even contemplating buying a property in Italy without legal advice. The bottom line is, you will know your own appetite for risk. If you don't speak Italian and do not know the house-buying process in Italy, you will probably be happier and safer having someone independent to advise you.

Appointing a surveyor

On a similar note, you will also have to decide if you want to appoint a surveyor and commission a structural report on your house before signing anything. The nature of many Italian properties – the fact that they are ruins – will often make such a report superfluous. You do not need a qualified surveyor to tell you the property is not watertight when you can see that there is no roof and that the walls are falling down. However, a surveyor, architect or builder could give you a ballpark figure for the price of restoration, which could be useful. If the property is habitable (and is priced accordingly), and you want to be certain about its condition, a surveyor's report will be a good investment.

The *compromesso di vendita*

Once you have agreed a price you and the vendor will sign a *compromesso di vendita* (promise to buy). The *compromesso* is the single most important document when buying a house in Italy, more important than the final contract, and you must not sign it unless you understand everything that is written on it. This contract is a legally binding document and describes the property to be sold and the land that comes with it. The land is identified in numbered lots called *particelle*. The contract gives details of the purchase price, names of the buyer and the vendor, the predicted date for the completion of the sale and the name of the *notaio* or notary who will take care of all the formalities. At the end of the *compromesso* there is space for you to insert conditional clauses. For example, in our *compromesso* we listed agricultural equipment that we wanted to remain on the property and we also stipulated that it was the vendor's responsibility to get permission for a barn to be de-ruralized – registered as no longer being for agricultural use and therefore applicable for conversion into habitable accommodation. For her part, the woman who sold us the house specified that she wanted that year's production of olive oil but would give us 20 litres as a gift. You can, therefore, put in whatever clauses you like. Note that the *compromesso* is in Italian, usually on a standard printed form with your particular details typed or written by hand. As this is the basis of the purchase contract, it is at this point before you sign it that you will have to decide if you want a lawyer or independent adviser to look at it. Remember – it is crucial to understand all the terms of the *compromesso*. Once the *compromesso* has been signed you and the vendor are legally committed to the sale, as defined in the document.

The deposit

At this stage you will be asked to hand over a *caparra* (deposit) of 10–30 per cent. The amount of the deposit will vary – for example, it may be that the vendor needs a larger amount to pay off the existing mortgage before the completion date. If you withdraw after signing the *compromesso* you will lose your deposit. The vendor can also withdraw but would have to pay double the deposit as a penalty. It is rare, but not unknown, for this to happen. It might occur, for example, if you have put down the minimum deposit and the vendor receives a much higher offer for the property so he can afford to pay the double penalty.

Proposta irrevocabile d'acquisto

There is an alternative contract that is used on rare occasions but does not replace the *compromesso*. This is a *proposta irrevocabile d'acquisto* (an irrevocable proposal to buy, subject to contract). Despite its name, this contract is not legally binding and does not mean that you have secured the property. What the *proposta* does is let the vendor know that you intend to buy and to sign a *compromesso* at a future date. It is a lure so that he will take the house off the market and not show it to other prospective buyers. Perhaps you need time to get your finance in place

– that is when a *proposta* could be useful. There will be a time limit to this agreement, normally 15 to 30 days, and you will pay a nominal deposit – say, 1,000 euros. If the vendor is approached by someone who offers a higher asking price, he can terminate the agreement and go with the second buyer. Your small deposit should be returned but there is no guarantee. If you decide to pull out, the vendor will probably keep the money as some kind of compensation.

Between the signing of the *compromesso* and the final *atto*, you will need a *codice fiscale*, similar to a National Insurance number, so that you can open a bank account to transfer funds for the complete payment on the house and for tax collection purposes (see the section on red tape).

Notaio

The estate agent or your adviser will have already recommended the name of a *notaio* and may have suggested that the *compromesso* is signed in his presence. The *notaio* is a public official responsible for completing the sale, collecting the taxes and registering the transfer of the property. The *notaio* is there to check on behalf of the state that all the boxes are ticked. Notaios are not there to represent either the buyer or the vendor, only to act as a witness for both sides. They will not, for example, check that you are paying a fair price or that the contract is in your best interests. A notaio and his or her staff, however, should personally carry out all the conveyancing work. This includes verifying that:

▌ The property is the vendor's to sell and that other members of the family do not have claims on the house or land.

▌ The property is not part of a contested will.

▌ The property does not have any encumbrances such as a prior mortgage or unpaid taxes.

▌ The property is not subject to any *servitu'* or *diritti di passaggi* – rights of way (some of these will be permanent and irrevocable while others can be withdrawn). He does this by going to the archives to look at the previous *compromessi* for your house and your neighbours' houses.

▌ The property is as described on the old land registry (*catasto*) and the house is registered at the new urban registry. If this latter registration has not been done by the vendor (and quite often with old farm properties this will be the case), then there is an obligation on the purchaser to register the property within a year of purchase.

A *notaio* should be scrupulous in these checks and confirm everything to his or her own satisfaction. However, as with all professions, some people are more scrupulous than others. Some *notaios* merely take the word of an estate agent or a lawyer on trust – especially if they know them and work with them regularly. If the bulk of the conveyancing work is left in the hands of the estate agent you need to be mindful of the conflict of interests that will undoubtedly exist. Usually, the estate agent acts for both buyer and seller and is paid by both. It is common for this to be the same percentage (say 3 per cent) from both parties. As the estate agent will not be paid any fee if the transaction does not go ahead, it is in his or her best interests to minimize any problems (see cautionary tales, below).

Atto di acquisto

The date for the final contract (*atto di acquisto*) will have been written in the *compromesso* – there is usually a two to three month space between signing the *compromesso* and this last hurdle, but this is something to be negotiated between you and the vendor. The final contracts must be exchanged in the *notaio's* office – this can prove to be quite a formal occasion with two official witnesses, buyer, vendor and all the other parties involved. When we signed our final contract we were led into the *notaio's* wood-panelled office and were shown to two very grand, red velvet chairs in the centre of the room while all the other witnesses were grouped around us. It felt like we were getting married in a register office instead of buying a house.

The *notaio* will read out loud the *atto* (the deeds of sale) so that both sides are clear about what is being bought and sold. If you are not fluent in Italian, the law demands that an interpreter is present to translate for you and to give you a copy of the deed in your own language.

The *atto* lists a description of the buildings and property for sale, the names of the buyer and vendor and the declared value of the property, which is not necessarily the purchase price.

Declared value

The declared value is used to calculate property tax for both the buyer and the vendor and is based on *catasto* (land registry) price tables. The practice of under-declaring the value of a property seems strange but is regarded as an acceptable legal loop-hole and is commonplace in Italy. Some *notaios* leave the room or take a telephone call when this matter is being agreed and understandably foreign buyers find it difficult to comprehend and feel uncomfortable with it. An under-valuation is normal practice, but you need to understand the implications.

Using the actual purchase price would feel more natural to most foreign buyers. However, there are pros and cons. Using the purchase price will mean that you and the vendor will have to pay more tax at the point of sale and you may find this is something you have to reach in the negotiation on the purchase price. In addition, as all future property taxes are based on this figure, these will also be set at a high rate.

If you set the declared value too far below the purchase price the authorities could question the valuation and reassess the value of the property at a higher figure. You could be fined and made to pay the shortfall in the taxes.

There is also a risk that when you come to sell the house the potential buyer will not agree to an under-declaration and you may have to pay tax on the difference between the price at which you declared you bought the house and that at which you sell it. In addition, as the valuation is lodged at the *catasto* it is viewed as the price you paid for the house. Therefore, if for some reason your house is compulsorily purchased – some unforeseen land development or someone exercising their pre-emption rights (see cautionary tales) – they would only have to compensate you for the declared value. In fact, in the case of someone exercising their pre-emption rights, they would also need to compensate you for any materials you had used on rebuilding or refurbishing the house, but not, unfortunately, any labour costs.

So the main message is, if you agree to an under-declaration it is in your interests to make sure the figure is realistic. A significant under-declaration might sound attractive in terms of keeping the overall cost of the purchase transaction low, but it will leave you in a very exposed position if any problems occur at a later date. The general rule of thumb seems to be that it is safe to declare 50 to 60 per cent of the value. Your estate agent or adviser will give you guidance on this.

Property ownership

Italian law recognizes two forms of property ownership – *communione di beni* and *separazione di beni*. Basically, this means that you can choose with your spouse or partner if your property is owned jointly or separately. The notary will explain these options to you and it will be noted on the final contract. Once the transaction has been completed the *notaio* will register the deeds within 21 days. It may be some time before you receive your copy of the registered title deed, so chase it up if it doesn't appear.

The costs

The costs of buying a house in Italy are higher than in the UK and many other European countries. I recall my estate agent going through the list of expenses associated with buying the property and I thought it sounded endless. In fact, the total cost of buying a house ends up at 15–17 per cent of the purchase price. You will have to pay:

■ Purchase tax – 10 per cent of the declared price if the property is urban and you are non-resident in Italy, or 19 per cent on agricultural property. This tax comes down to 3 per cent if you are resident or say you will become resident within 18 months of signing the final contract. If you say you will become resident and then either don't or do but sell the house within 5 years without buying another one in Italy within 2 years, the state has the right to claw-back the 7 per cent difference.

■ Notaio's fee – 1 to 2.5 per cent of the declared price.

■ *Bolli* (stamp duty) – 1 per cent of the declared price.

You will also have to pay estate agency fees of 3 to 6 per cent of the purchase price, plus IVA. In addition there may be legal or advisory fees, translation and survey costs.

Power of attorney

If you are not able to be present in Italy for the *atto*, you can give the power of attorney (*procura*) to a nominated representative (normally your adviser or legal representative) and they will sign on your behalf. This will cost in the region of 200 euros.

The purchase of an apartment in a condominium

Living in an apartment in a *condominio* is commonplace in Italy. Each person in the block of flats owns his or her apartment and is co-owner with the other flat-owners of the common parts of the building. The common parts will include the structure of the building, the land on which the building stands, the entrance halls and corridors, the drains, the heating and hot water system and the elevator. If you are in a holiday resort and there are shared leisure facilities such as a swimming pool or a tennis court, this is also included under joint ownership.

These properties are cheaper and offer more security than a lone dwelling. Many second home owners like them because ownership is less onerous – they can lock up their apartment, return home and do not have to worry about maintenance. However, there are drawbacks. You will be living at close quarters with lots of other people, so lack of privacy may be an issue. Italians are not the quietest of people and you may be bothered by noise. You may be banned from keeping pets or, conversely, be annoyed by other people's dogs barking in the middle of the night.

Do not think about buying an apartment without using a *notaio*, a lawyer or another independent adviser because buying *condominio* property is much more complicated than buying a single house. The contracts are difficult to understand and need to be thoroughly checked. You and your adviser will want to see the *condominio* agreement, which sets out the rights and responsibilities of each flat-owner and the service charges (*spese*) you will be expected to pay. The estate agent selling you the apartment, or the developer if this is a new block, will have this document.

You should also try to talk to someone who already lives in the block and try to get an assessment from them about what it is like to live there. Examine the building and if you see obvious signs of wear and tear, ask the seller if any major expenses are likely to be required in the future. Ask about the central heating and hot water system. Is it shared or does everyone pay for their own supply? If there is a shared system, and this will be your holiday home and you are not often there, you would end up paying for hot water and heating that you do not use. Note: shared central heating and hot water usually only applies to old properties. New properties in Italy now have individual systems.

Depending on the size and position of the flat in the block, you will have a proportion of the common parts *(l'ente condominiale)*. Garages, parking places and cantinas will also be counted as part of your overall property. These proportions govern the service charge – if you live in a three bedroom flat with a garage and a cantina you will pay more *spese* than a neighbour who lives in a one bedroom apartment. Tenants who live on the ground floor are not normally asked to contribute to the running costs of the elevator service.

Most condominiums in Italy now have an *amministratore di condominio* who manages the property on the tenants' behalf. He will be responsible for ensuring the property is kept in good condition, carrying out necessary repairs, collecting *spese* and dealing with complaints. Obviously, some managing agents will be more efficient than others. If you do have a complaint, put it in writing and send it by registered mail so that you know the managing agent has received it.

The tenants of a *condominio* will meet once or twice a year to discuss the general business of the building. Every flat-owner must be informed of this meeting and is entitled to vote, according to the number of shares he or she has, on matters such as refurbishment, installing alarm systems, changing insurance companies, etc. If you cannot be there in person you can give your votes to a proxy who may attend the meeting on your behalf. You could choose a neighbour you trust, a friend from outside the *condominio,* or a legal adviser.

Cautionary tales

Through my own experience, and the experience of friends who have bought houses in Italy, I have collected a number of cautionary tales. These stories are not meant to scare the living daylights out of prospective property buyers or to be a definitive list of all the things that can go wrong. They merely illustrate some of the things that can happen. We came to see these problems as part of our baptism into Italian culture, something to laugh about once they were safely resolved.

Pre-emption rights *(prelazione)*

Prelazione is the right of a neighbouring farmer to buy the property that you are intending to purchase. If he makes 70 per cent or more of his income from agriculture or agro-tourism, he has priority to buy over you. This is a very sensible safeguard for maintaining viable farming communities in Italy. *Prelazione* can be exercised up to two years after the sale of the property and is therefore one of the trickiest parts of buying a property in Italy. Prior to buying a house you will need to check whether your neighbours have *prelazione* and if they want to exercise them. In a simple world, this would mean writing to the neighbour setting out the details of the property sale (it is important to note that this must be the value that is going to be declared – otherwise the exercise is invalidated) and giving them 30 days to declare whether they wish to exercise their rights. However, life is often far from simple. It is not necessarily easy or straightforward to find out who are your potential neighbours. Italian inheritance laws mean that land is often divided up into quite small parcels and/or is jointly owned by a large number of family members. In addition, properties will often be sold with a number of non-contiguous land parcels. A friend of mine who was buying 22 acres in Marche found he had 78 registered neighbours. His lawyer pointed that even if he despatched 78 letters and waited 30 days, there was a significant risk that the Italian postal service would let them down and someone would declare that they never received the notification. An alternative would be to demand a response from each, confirming that the letter had been received. However, there is no legal requirement for the neighbour to do this and therefore it would not be enough to get round the problem. Another possible solution was to ask all those parties with *prelazione* to attend the final signing of the contract at which stage they sign away their rights on the contract. My friend flirted with this idea but then decided 78 neighbours (plus their relatives) turning up to the signing ceremony could become a logistical nightmare – if indeed the neighbours could agree on a date for the contract. In fact in his case the matter was taken out of his hands. One of the 78 heard a deal was in hand, came forward, and exercised his rights. My friend was left with a legal bill for £2,000 and was back to square one.

In our own case we were three days from signing the final contract when our estate agent dropped into the conversation that there was 'a small problem' on the horizon. He told us that we could still buy the house but that he now suggested that we should rent the land on which it was standing for two years. At the end of that period we would be able to complete the purchase. We went berserk, of course, and said that this was not a small problem: this was nuclear. He tried describing the situation over the phone but it was hopeless – mobiles are never good at the best of times and trying to understand in Italian what appeared to be a complex legal setback was impossible. We were in London at the time but took the next flight over to Italy. It took hours to understand the nature of this so-called problem by which time my hair was turning white and my husband was all for buying a house in Dorset. But the essence of the situation was this: the woman who was selling us the house had had a stormy, indeed litigious, relationship with the nearest neighbours. On this basis she thought it was unlikely they would sign away their *prelazione* rights, and because they were no longer on speaking terms there was no way for this to be confirmed. My agent, who was also acting for the seller, tried to think of a way of overcoming the situation and in doing so, came up with the ridiculous idea of leaving the land in the vendor's name so that the rights could not be exercised. Having rented 'our' land for two years we would then have the right to buy. The agent – who wanted to push through the sale – was very pleased with his solution and failed to see why we should have any fears about buying the house under these conditions. 'So we can buy this house but as soon as we step outside our front door, we'll be walking on rented land?' we asked. He still couldn't see why we were uneasy and promised us that the arrangement would be watertight.

We decided the only way forward was to actually meet the neighbours and establish whether they did want to buy our property. We didn't, in any case, want to live near people who might resent us. (This is one of the reasons why you should meet your neighbours in advance of a sale, if possible.) We all went along to their house and discovered not only did they have no interest in our future home, they were terribly nice people and were thrilled at the idea of having new people come to live on the hillside. Of course they would sign whatever we wanted, whenever we wanted them to. Problem solved. Easily. This illustrates what I now see as a national trait in Italians, of over-complicating things. Quite often they approach issues assuming there will be problems when in reality none exist. A year or so later, we discovered from our neighbours, who are now good friends, that all of the drama had been for nothing. They didn't have *prelazione* rights in the first place – no one had actually asked them. They had signed the contract to make us feel secure and to ensure that the previous owner didn't stay on. What was the renting thing all about – I don't suppose we'll ever know.

Have a survey done

There are many instances when people – and obviously this problem is not confined to Italy – discover after purchase that they have 'been sold a pup'. An acquaintance of mine and her husband made the decision to purchase a renovated house, rather than a ruin, as they were planning to move to Italy immediately with two young children and another on the way. The house had been beautifully restored by an Italian couple who had used it as a weekend retreat. The new people moved in just before Christmas and within two days the water 'ran out'. They had been told the house had access to mains water and they discovered that what they had was in fact a 750 litre plastic *cisterna* in one of the cantinas – this didn't last long with a whole family washing, showering, etc. Having accepted she would have to throw money at the problem and have a connection to the mains installed, my acquaintance then struggled to find anyone prepared to undertake the work in mid-winter. It was spring before the work could be done and in the meantime the family survived on a mixture of water tank deliveries and trips to the local fountain. She also said that she could heartily recommend the showering facilities at the local swimming pool!

That, unfortunately, was not the end of the problems. One day, on flushing the toilet, the whole system seemed to have backed up. After clearing up the mess she called someone in to look at the septic tank. She had been told it was under the lawn in front of the house and in fact the vendors had walked round the area with them to illustrate where it was. First a man with a shovel arrived and dug a hole in the right place but could find no sign of it. So it was decided it must have been buried deeper. A man with a bulldozer arrived to complete the job quickly. After he had destroyed the entire lawn it became clear there was no tank, the pipes from the house just ended – abruptly. Although this explained why the lawn had grown so well during the drought, it was little comfort to her. She had to fork out for a complete sewage system to be installed (before replanting the lawn). Would a survey have identified these problems? My feeling is that a surveyor would have instantly known the *cisterna* was not being fed from the mains supply. The problem of the non-existent septic tank might have been harder to spot and it was just plain bad luck that the vendors had been so deceitful.

Check professional credentials

You can run into problems even if you have employed professional help. Another friend, who is currently undertaking a renovation of a dilapidated farmhouse, employed an architect to draw up the designs before finding a *geometra* to take over the works as building manager. The *geometra* submitted the plans to the local *comune* for authorization and several months later returned them to my friend, duly stamped up and ready to go. In the early stages of the building work someone from the *comune* passed by and asked why planning permission had not been sought. Having seen the endorsed plans he disappeared only to return the next day confirming that the plans had never been endorsed, but merely held and then stamped by the *geometra*. A very Italian solution resulted. The official who had originally identified the problem then bent over backwards to find a way around the problem, the *geometra* just shrugged his shoulders (it is not clear if the Italian authorities will seek to punish him in any way) and the building work was merely delayed for a few days. This story illustrates another point: while pretty horrendous problems can turn up, the Italians usually find a way to circumvent them and indeed seem to relish the challenge.

6 Banking and mortgages

There is a bewildering number of banks in Italy. Many of them are small savings or regional banks. Do not open an account in one of these small establishments unless you are absolutely certain that you will remain in that area. For example, a friend of mine opened an account with the Cassa di Risparmio di Lucca when he was buying a house in Tuscany. The sale of the house fell through and when he bought another property in Marche he discovered that his bank did not have any branches in that part of Italy so it was pretty useless trying to cash cheques or withdraw money. He had to close the first bank account and transfer to a new one – there was a lot of paperwork involved and it was a tedious complication.

The biggest banking groups are Banca Intesa Bci, Banca di S Paolo IMI, Monte Dei Paschi Di Siena and UniCredito. The Banca D'Italia is the only bank authorized to issue euro notes in Italy. The smaller banks are either independent or affiliated to the larger groups.

As a foreigner you can open an Italian bank account whether you are resident or not. You will need to present a *codice fiscale* and your passport when you are filling in the application. Non-residents are limited to a *conto estero*. You receive a blue-coloured *libretto di assegni* (chequebook) with 10 cheques. You can also apply for a *bancomat* card, a debit payment card that is widely accepted in Italy and can be used pretty much everywhere, from hardware stores to supermarkets. You type a personal code (*codice segreto*) into the shop's machine and no signature is required. You can also use your *bancomat* to withdraw money from cash machines. You will be restricted to a certain amount of cash withdrawals each month using your *bancomat* – an average sum is 3,500 euros. If you exceed that limit and need to withdraw more, you will have to go into the bank and withdraw cash direct from the bank teller.

You can have bank statements, which are issued either monthly or quarterly, sent to your address abroad. Many banks provide English translations of accounts, although the language and grammar one somewhat strangulated. Most foreigners keep the absolute minimum amount in their *conto estero,* using it only to pay bills and general living expenses, but make sure you do not inadvertently become overdrawn. If there is a danger of this you should let the bank know in advance and ask their indulgence, because unauthorized overdrafts are frowned upon.

If you are a resident you can open a bank account like any Italian. You can also apply for credit cards. There is no problem having any account in joint names with your partner.

Bank services can seem erratic to foreigners. You can spend a good half hour on even the simplest transaction. In my bank people queue haphazardly for the tellers so you never know who is first in line, and the computers seem to crash or go slow quite regularly. Others have automated ticket systems and you have to wait in line. It is a good idea to try to develop a personal relationship with someone at your bank – perhaps the person (*il gestore*) who helped you open the account. They have probably helped other foreigners open accounts, will be able to speak a bit of English and will be able to answer all your questions. Utilities such as telephone, electricity, etc, should be paid by direct debit so that you are not cut off while you are away, and bank staff are usually very helpful in assisting you to fill in the forms. The charge for each direct debit is 80 cents.

Cheque accounts are interest-bearing but the rate is normally only 0.5 per cent. Many people do not date cheques when they write them because interest is withheld on the account from the date a cheque is written and not on the day it is presented to the bank. This is an important consideration if you are paying a builder a large amount by cheque, for example. Cheques may have to be endorsed on the back and they can be transferred to a third person, so you may have to write *non-trasferibile* on the front. Interest rates on savings accounts are 2 to 4 per cent on average.

Allow plenty of time for transfers of money from abroad – friends of mine opened an account with their local bank and were expecting a sum of 80,000 euros to arrive as final payment for their house purchase. They waited and waited, going into the bank every day, and still nothing arrived. When the day of the *atto* arrived they were desperately worried and asked the bank what they should do. They had already shown a photocopy from their own bank in the US saying that the money had been sent off. The manager shrugged his shoulders, said he was sure the money was in transit somewhere, and arranged for them to have 80,000 euros credit so that they could complete the purchase. My friends had only recently opened this account and they were not particularly well known to the bank manager – but hey, that's one of the glories of Italy. There are rules but they are made to be broken and sometimes they can be in your favour.

Bank hours vary according to each bank, but as a general rule they are open from 8.30am until 1.30pm and from 3pm until 4 or 4.30pm, Mondays to Fridays. As a foreigner, try not to go during the busy early morning period because you will feel self-conscious trying to explain what you want, with lots of interested Italian customers listening in!

Transferring money to Italy

There are no restrictions on transferring money to Italy. You can make transfers easily from your home account into your Italian account using an IBAN number, which means you can transfer money from the UK without being charged at the receiving bank. Your bank in the UK will normally take five working days to transfer money, but you can pay an extra fee and have the money sent within one working day. To take money out of Italy – for example, if you have sold your house and want to transfer the proceeds – you should consult an accountant *(commercialista* or *ragioniere)* to advise you on the most practical way to do this. In line with all European financial establishments, Italian banks have a duty to combat money laundering and are likely to ask questions about significant sums of money being moved around. They may ask for proof of what you are spending it on.

Mortgages

A mortgage is called a *mutuo* or *ipoteca* in Italy. You can seek a mortgage through an Italian bank or international credit company. Alternatively, you may want to go with a British-owned building society, bank or credit company. The advantage of this, of course, is that all dealings and documentation are in English. Whatever kind of finance house you deal with, try to arrange a mortgage 'in principle,' as you would do if you were buying a property in the UK. In this way you can start searching for your Italian property, confident in how much money you can spend. Note that purchasers are expected to put down at least a 20 per cent deposit themselves. All mortgage lenders assess eligibility in largely the same way. Loans need to be supported through proof of income – if employed, you must present your employment contract, copies of your last three months' payslips and copies of your latest P60/Employer's Reference together with copies of your last six months' bank statements. If you are self-employed you must present copies of your last three years' accounts, copies of the last 12 months' business and last six months' personal bank statements, and the last two years' tax returns. Some lenders ask for a covering letter from your accountant, confirming your personal financial situation.

The loan is calculated on an affordability basis. Existing mortgage/rent payments, personal loans, credit card debts and any maintenance commitments – these payments together with your proposed Italian mortgage payments must not exceed 35 per cent of your net monthly income. Lenders are unlikely to take into consideration any proposed rental income from your property as part of the affordability calculation.

Italian lenders used to be wary about offering mortgages to foreigners, but the situation has changed enormously in the past decade because of the sheer numbers of non-Italians buying property. Banks recognized that this was a business opportunity going to waste and with some lenders you can now get a yes/no in principle for an Italian mortgage over the telephone.

Italian lenders only offer repayment mortgages – endowment and pension-linked mortgages do not exist – with interest and capital being repaid in equal instalments for the duration of the mortgage. Mortgages will have a fixed or variable interest rate and there is a maximum loan of 85 per cent for a first home (for residents) or 90 per cent if you can prove you are doing a lot of restoration work, and 50 or 60 per cent for second homes (for non-residents). Loans are generally repaid quicker than in your home country – a 5 to 20-year term is normal, but you can find mortgages for up to 30 years. All mortgages must be repaid by the age of 70 and must be supported by life cover. Italian lenders will take first charge over your mortgaged property as security for the loan.

Interest rates are very competitive. I heard of one Italian bank offering a rate of 1.9 per cent for the first year and a fixed or variable rate after that.

In general, mortgage rates seem to be between 3 and 4 per cent. Mortgage offers are made in writing and have a time limit of 30 days for acceptance.

Some people feel happier taking out a loan with a British lender. The Woolwich offers loans for an Italian property of up to 80 per cent. The Italia side of Abbey National, which is now owned by UniCredito Italiano, offers loans of up to 85 per cent and a licensed credit broker such as Conti Financial Services offers 80 per cent. Again, your monthly outgoings plus proposed Italian mortgage payments should not exceed 35 per cent of your net monthly income. CFS, a member of FOPDAC (Federation of Overseas Property Developers Agents and Consultants) gives this example:

> Net joint monthly income £2,500 times 35 per cent of that figure is £875 minus existing monthly mortgage payment £300 – no other liabilities. This leaves a balance of £575 for a proposed Italian mortgage payment.

Another option is to raise the finance in the UK by using your prime residence as security. You can ask your mortgage lender to increase your existing mortgage facility or take out a second mortgage – but be sure to get good advice before you go down this route.

Supporting documents

When you apply for a mortgage, whether it is from an Italian lender or one in your home country, you will need to provide the following documents:

- photocopies of passport, birth, marriage or divorce certificate;
- last six months' personal bank statements;
- *codice fiscale* if resident in Italy and/or proof of residency in your home country – domestic bills with your name and address usually suffice.

As mentioned above, you will also need to show proof of income.

Property details

You will also be required to supply comprehensive information about your Italian home. This will include: copy of the *compromesso*, proof of the deposit you have paid on the house and an estimate of the price of renovations if you are applying for a mortgage to cover these costs.

Photographs showing the work to be done and an architect's or *geometra's* report will also be useful.

Costs

The lender will expect you to pay 250 euros for an official valuation of the property and commission will be 0.5 per cent to 1 per cent of the total amount of the loan. If you are using a non- Italian lender, you will have to pay the same commission plus an arrangement fee of approximately £250.

Restoring a property

Friends of ours bought a wonderful *casale rustico* in the Italian countryside and employed a team of local builders to restore it. At the beginning of the project the stonemasons, carpenters and plumbers were driving battered old Fiats; by the time the house is finished they were zooming around in Alfa Romeos while their *capo* was at the wheel of a top-of-the-range BMW. 'We paid for all those cars', our friends said glumly.

The biggest fear people have during a restoration project is of being ripped off. Although he was an extremely successful businessman in the UK, the husband feels that he failed to manage the budget for the restoration of the property. He spent too much and it still leaves a bitter taste in his mouth. In fact, it has ruined a lot of the pleasure he should have had from his magnificent home.

How can you keep control of the building costs? You are, after all, in a foreign country and have probably never re-built a house like this before. There are steps you can take to minimize the financial risks and ensure the restoration is done to your taste.

Choosing an architect or designer

If it is a complete restoration you will need an architect or interior designer to help you. The condition of the house you have bought will dictate which one it will be – if the property is more or less a ruin and has to be re-built from scratch, an architect who is experienced in structural design will be necessary. If the house needs less structural work but complete re-modelling, then an interior designer could be the person you are after. You must decide if you are going to use an Italian or find someone from home. The local chap will do what he knows and understands, and that might be a project that is quite conservative and provincial. For example, you could get a bathroom next to a kitchen or a corridor with lots of bedrooms running off it. Italians also struggle to accept the idea of imperfection and can take the character out of an Italian home, making the end product look like the inside of a Barratt house in Essex.

If you choose an architect or designer from your own country, you will have someone who is more likely to be in tune with your tastes, as well as someone with whom you can discuss in your own language your hopes and dreams. You will have to pay for him to fly out to Italy perhaps half a dozen times during the restoration project, but if you are already spending a lot of money it might be worthwhile to do this. Believe it or not, it does not require a lot of words to instruct a builder properly, so a lack of Italian is not necessarily a problem. Whoever you choose, meet him and see if you get on. If you don't – dump him. It is always better to withdraw, even if you have met up several times, and admit that you will not work well together, than to look back at the end of a project and say: 'That was a mistake.'

Budget and talking the same visual language

Never worry that your project might be too small. Even the most successful architect or designer will find it difficult to refuse the challenge of re-building your home in Italy. What you have to ascertain is what it will cost you and whether he is happy to work to your budget. If he does, ask to see projects he has completed, speak to previous clients and see if they were satisfied with his work. Make sure you have the same tastes. Look at magazines, tear out pictures of houses that you like, try to draw your own ideas. You need to know that you are both talking the same visual language, not just the same words – and there is a world of difference. It is probably best to choose someone with a track record so that you know the project is within his capabilities. A new and untried graduate may seem a cheap option, but will he know how to pull you out of the mud? He might.

You could also choose to work with one of the British estate agents/renovators already resident in Italy. They have restored other Italian houses, will have building teams that they use regularly and can supervise the project on your behalf. Again, this will be an extra cost but it could save you a great deal of time and worry. Of course, if you are fabulously stylish and confident about what you are doing, you can be your own architect/designer, but choosing a professional will mean that you can be more adventurous in the re-design of your house. Alone, you will be tempted to play safe and you could miss out on a once-in-a-lifetime opportunity to do something really special with your Italian home. In our case, we chose a friend who was an interior designer to help us with our house and he encouraged us to be much braver in our design than we would have been if we had been left to our own devices.

It is a good idea to do some of this work in advance of buying your house in Italy so that you can take your chosen person to look at the site and to advise you whether it is a practical project within your time frame and budget. This will give you a second opinion that is usually more accurate than the views of friends and relatives. If you choose an Italian architect, ask if they belong to the *Ordine degli Architetti.* The Royal Institute of British Architects in London can help with recommendations in the UK.

Geometra

You will need a *geometra*. This man is a very important figure. He is not a taste, style or fashion consultant: he is the man who will see that your house is built, restored on time, on budget and legally. This is the beginning of a team effort and it is essential your architect/designer and *geometra* respect and like each other. The *geometra* will steer you through the peculiarities of Italian planning and will find you a team of local builders. He knows all the suppliers of sanitary ware, marble, wood and whatever else you need to do up your house. As ever, knowledge is power. Ask in your local town or village which *geometras* are well regarded – the person with the best reputation usually has it for a good reason. Go and see what he does and how he does it. Ask to speak to former clients and view examples of other houses he has worked on. Remember that he is there to do only what you want and to give you technical advice. On the other hand, it is his ability to find for you the best local people that will create the success of the project. Although all you finally see is the plaster and the coat of paint, what lies behind it will ensure that your house remains dry, stays warm and cool when required and keeps out the elements, smells and creatures.

The *geometra* liaises with the *comune* (the municipal authority that will approve or reject your building plans). Note that planning permission is required for swimming pools, and even for making changes to the levels of your land, so there will be a lot of paperwork involved. He will know all the important people in all the various committees and can work on your behalf to get around building regulations. If your house is listed as historic he will have to consult the *Belle Arte*, the equivalent of English Heritage, to see what work will be permitted and what building materials must be used. He will check your architect's or designer's drawings to confirm that they correspond to local building rules. He will do all the paperwork and payments. He is part chartered surveyor, part on-site foreman and general engineer. As a foreigner, you cannot do without him so make sure you employ someone in whom you have confidence.

Preventivo

The *geometra* will go to your house, inspect it, look at your building plans and draw up a list of the work that has to be done *(capitolato d'appalto)*. This can range from pulling the whole lot down and re-building it completely to replacing wooden beams and stonework, converting the *stalle* downstairs into living accommodation, re-plumbing, re-wiring, installing bathrooms and a kitchen. This list may run to 20 or so pages and will be a valuable reference guide for you as the project goes along. It will be in Italian, so get your dictionary out and start translating the main headings. It is a lot of work but not difficult and it is essential you understand this document.

He will distribute the list to three or four local builders and ask them for an estimate *(un preventivo)*. The builders will itemize everything by cost, giving a final figure and a start time for building work. They will also give a date for the completion of the project. When the estimates are back, it is up to you to decide which building team to use. Talk to your architect and *geometra* – there is unlikely to be a huge disparity in prices, but some builders may not be able to start for a year or so.

Choosing a builder

Again, you have to do research when deciding which builder to use. Go and speak to the one you are interested in. Ask him to take you to the site he is currently working on. Is it tidy and well ordered? Do his men seem to be working quietly and efficiently? Are they part of a regular, local gang or does he use casual labour? It is bad working practice to have casual workers coming and going. Ask to see a house similar to yours that the builder has already restored. Look for quality not cheapness. Are the walls straight? Are the tiles in the bathroom level and properly grouted? If you can, interview the builder's previous clients. One of the most important things to ask is whether their project came in on time and on budget. Did they find the builder amenable and easy to work with? What things went wrong and what things went right? If you do not speak Italian, you will also have to consider how good the communication is between you and the prospective builder. Do you think you can all understand each other with only basic conversations, drawings and diagrams? If not, you can find someone to act as translator although this is, of course, an added expense.

Use local builders if you can

In Tuscany, Umbria and Marche at the present time, demand for builders is high and many are booked up months ahead. Some *geometras* will recommend using building gangs from outside the region. For example, builders from Puglia are being used in Marche. There is nothing intrinsically wrong with this, but what if something goes wrong when the house is finished and your builders are then hundreds of miles away? It is best to use local labour if you can.

Building contract

Once you have chosen your builder, you will both sign a *contratto di appalto* (building contract) and you must agree a payment schedule. If a building is being completely restored, you are obviously not going to pay all the costs up front – it is normal to put down a deposit and then make a payment every month or two months for the duration of the building works. Most *geometras* will put in a time clause on the building contract – if the work is not finished in time the builder pays a penalty. It is acceptable to hold back about 10 per cent of the total cost for a few months in case any problems with the building work emerge. You should have this written into your building contract.

Hidden costs

A word of warning about *preventivos*. Problems about money surface when the list of tasks to be done is incomplete. Some *geometras* or builders do not make an accurate assessment of all the work that is to be done. They may even deliberately leave important things out so that the *preventivo* comes in at an attractively low price. The problems are then 'revealed' halfway through the building process and you have to find extra money to cover them. A good *preventivo* should be accurate – at the end of the job you should pay no more than 5 or 10 per cent extra, to account for genuine hidden problems that may be uncovered during a restoration. Ask your *geometra* what costs are not included. For example, you will have to pay a fee to the central heating engineer. You will have to pay for sanitary ware for the bathrooms. You may have to pay additional costs for connecting electricity or gas supplies. If you are putting in new doors, you have to pay for them and for the door furniture – handles, locks, etc. If the *preventivo* is too high, you and your architect should ask the *geometra* where it is possible to cut costs.

Keep your own records

From the beginning of your restoration project, keep notes. During and after every meeting with your architect/designer, *geometra* or builder, write down all the salient points that have been discussed. There is so much to remember during a building project – especially if a lot of it is conducted in Italian – that you really do need an *aide-memoire* so that you can go back and refer to different points if necessary. For example, the builder may say that you didn't tell him that you wanted a particular colour of plaster on the walls. If you have notes of that meeting, you can put him right. This kind of diary also makes a nice souvenir of such a big and very personal undertaking. It won't be pretty – you will have scribbles and drawings all over it – but it will be invaluable. Buy a hard-backed notebook so that you use it all the time, instead of jotting down things on bits of paper or grotty notepads that will get lost. And, of course, take tons of photographs. Your house will change enormously and it is lovely to record its progress.

Communication

Clarity in your discussions with the building professionals is very important. You have to know at all times what you are agreeing to and they have to understand what you want. There is a bewildering amount of information to take in and it is easy to feel you are getting lost and that the project is running away with you. During our re-building, I used to sabotage myself all the time by saying 'Si, si…' during discussions. What I was doing was trying to translate everything really quickly in my head and digest all that was being said, but the builders naturally thought that I was saying that I understood the conversation. You are trying to comprehend Italian and they are trying to comprehend English. Misunderstandings can easily happen. We had a discussion about one of our internal walls, and each side thought the other side was clear about what was needed. When we returned a week later, the wall was in the wrong place. It was a small internal wall and it was no big deal to tear it down and re-build it in the right place, but it was an example of bad communication. You have to say in simple terms what you want and if you don't understand what someone is saying, get them to repeat it until you do. Don't be embarrassed. You are the client, you are paying the bills. You will be more confident in this if you have your own personal notes to consult.

Regular reports

The *geometra* and the builder should be willing to give you regular reports so that you can be kept informed of progress if you are able to visit Italy only once a month or so. They should also agree to take photographs or video film of important moments on-site, such as re-building the roof or installing pipe work so that you can see what is happening. It is frustrating when you return after several weeks away to find that important work has been carried out and is now covered in plaster or buried in the ground. The builder obviously cannot wait for you to arrive, so this is a good solution. Make it clear from the start, however, that if they uncover any new problems such as rotting beams they must inform you immediately and clear any extra costs with you.

Do not try to be friends with your building team in the hope that this will make your project go well. Friendship cannot be forced on either side. You want a professional relationship right from the start. Friendship will come if you get on well together as the project commences. Remember you are working in a foreign country. You want them to respect you and that means you must respect them. When dealing with the price for renovation, strike a hard bargain – but not a mean bargain. Haggle, but not too far. It is a delicate balance. Your architect or designer will be able to guide you, but the final decision is down to you.

Paying cash

This brings us to the debate about paying cash for some of the work. All work on properties in Italy is subject to IVA (VAT) at 10 per cent for restoration, preservation and restructuring works, and at 20 per cent on the purchase of building materials. If you pay in cash it means you can save this 10 or 20 per cent. This is a widespread practice because 'the black economy' is an acknowledged part of Italian life, but it means you will not have invoices for everything that has been done, therefore there needs to be a lot of trust between you and your building team before you consent to do this. It is another decision you will have to make for yourself by weighing up the pros and cons.

Do-It-Yourself

There will be DIY (*fai da te*) enthusiasts who are looking at houses with the view to working on the properties themselves. There is nothing wrong with this but be aware that you are dealing with very different kinds of buildings than, say, an apartment in London or a house in Glasgow. You are likely never to have worked with a house that has walls a metre thick or a living room that was once used to house cows and donkeys. Make sure that for essential work you hire or consult local labour to work alongside you or at least to give you advice and supplies.

Bringing out your own builder from your own country is not a good idea – and anyway, you should be patronizing local businesses. When you patronize local businesses, you make friends with the community. Remember that you will be creating a network of expertise that will see you in good stead for years to come. By creating alliances among local traders, and giving them your business, you become an accepted member of your local society. And when there is a foul smell coming from your *fossa biologica,* it is a lot easier to call the tradesman who lives 10 minutes down the road to come and fix it than to ask a plumber to jump on a plane.

The final weeks

Try to arrange your holidays from work so that you are at the house full-time in the final two or three weeks of building. This is when the project comes together, when your input will be needed most and there will be lots of things to decide upon.

Guarantees

If something goes wrong with your newly restored house you should be covered under a system called *piccoli danni/grande danni.* I say 'should be' because righting problems depends on being able to get back in touch with your builder. Obviously, you should have fewer problems if you use a large, reputable local firm. This means that if small things go wrong within two years, say for example that a new window leaks, the builder has to come back and fix it. You have a guarantee of 10 years for *grande danni* – if your newly constructed roof starts falling apart, for example.

Fees

Expect the following fees. An architect or designer will charge 10 to 15 per cent of the cost of the project, depending on how big the house is. A *geometra* will charge between 7 and 13 per cent of the total cost of the project – 10 per cent is the norm. The builder's fees are obviously included in the *preventivo*. You may also have to pay for someone to act as a translator at the beginning of the project or all the way through. As with all building work, unforeseen costs arise and you should keep aside an extra 10 to 20 per cent as a contingency fund.

8 Buying a new property or having a property built

More and more people are considering buying new properties in Italy and there is a lot to be said for walking into a brand-new apartment or villa where everything is clean and modern and you only need to choose the finish on your kitchen or bathroom. Whether you are buying from a developer or purchasing a plot of land and building from scratch, the same principle applies – check everything thoroughly before committing yourself by signing anything. Planning regulations will vary from region to region – some areas like Tuscany, for example, are more restrictive than others about what you are allowed to build.

Building plots

If you are going to buy a plot of land in Italy and build a new house from the ground up you will need to employ a *geometra* so that he can help you with all the checks that you will need to make. All land in Italy is classified for building purposes and there is a formula, which will vary with each region, about where you can build and the maximum size and height of the new house you can build. A *geometra* will be familiar with all the rules and regulations in his district and can advise you accordingly.

By and large, the situation is like this. Every *comune* has a *piano regolatore*, a large map of the surrounding area that shows the different zones for building purposes. This is an extremely detailed map of the area, its roads, public buildings and services and it is always available to the public for examination at the *ufficio piano regolatore* at your local *comune*. It also shows what changes are under way or planned – for example, if an extension of the motorway is about to be built or if a hospital or new train station is to be constructed.

The zones are:

▌ Zone A – the historic centre or *centro storico*. No new building is allowed here, you can only restore existing properties.

▌ Zone B – already urbanized. In sizeable Italian towns these zones will already be 80 or 90 per cent filled with new housing – and you can build in the unfilled spaces.

▌ Zone C – the expansion zone. These areas are generally large plots designated for building housing estates or apartment buildings but some may still be green field sites without solid plans for roads and sewage, etc. Therefore a very comprehensive project would have to be presented to the *comune* or *regione*.

▌ Zone D – industrial zone for factories, artisan workshops, etc.

▌ Zone E – the green zone or agricultural zone in the countryside where most of the traditional Italian farmhouses are sited. No new building is allowed – properties can be restored and expanded by a limited amount of space.

▌ Zone F – the service zone, for schools, hospitals, trains stations, etc.

Therefore, if you see a plot of land advertised for sale under *terreno edificabile* in an estate agency window or in a local newspaper, you and your adviser should look at where the land is sited on the *piano regolatore* and what zone it is in. If your plot of land is in a zone B, it may already be urbanized and ready to go. All you would have to do is submit detailed planning permission for the kind of house that you want to build and, if it is approved, work can begin relatively quickly. If your plot of land is in a zone C, it may also be ready to go or it may not yet be connected to the various services – gas, water, electricity and sewage. You might have to pay for connecting these services to the main networks or it may turn out that it is not viable for you to build a single house here.

The vendor of a building plot, if he is a lone individual, has no obligation to tell you if anything nasty is going to be built near your proposed house, so you must verify this yourself. Indeed, he might assure you that everything is fine in the hope that you are the kind of foreigner who will not check. He can plead innocence and say that he didn't actually know that a bypass for the motorway was being planned. Once you have bought a building plot it is very difficult to get redress so check everything out at the *comune*. The vendor also does not need to tell you if there is water on site if there is no mains supply. You will have to ask a *geologo* to carry out an inspection to see if a *pozzo* (well) can be dug and also to look at the sewage situation for your new house. If the plot is not connected to the main utilities, you need to check that there will not be any problems doing so, or putting in your own system and how much it will cost. As always, ask as many questions as you can, both of the vendor and of any neighbours who are around. Carry out as much research as possible before committing to buy.

You may want to employ an architect to draw up the plans of your house, although this will be an additional expense. An architect will charge approximately 10 to 15 per cent of the cost of the project. As with a restoration, you must find an architect who is in tune with your own tastes. Many Italians, perhaps because they have been brought up in draughty old houses in the country, go completely overboard when building a new villa. They install frankly ugly picture windows, paint the outside in lurid yellow or pink plaster and erect grand stone gates with lions on top at the entrance to the property. These houses are luxurious – some will have summer and winter kitchens, for example – but they are not very elegant. Monstrous carbuncles on the idyllic Italian landscape, as our *Principe Carlo* would say. Try to find an architect who will design you a house that will be in sympathy with your surroundings, not fighting against it.

Another option is to go for a builder who offers a standard range of properties where you can choose the internal specifications. If you are thinking about this, go and see examples of what has already been built. Be daring, knock on a door and ask if you can see inside – many Italians will be happy to show you around. You can also ask them questions about what they like and don't like about their new houses.

When the detailed plans for the house are drawn up, they will be submitted to the *comune* for permission to start work. A *capitolato d'appalto* (list of all the essential works) will also be drawn up and, if you are going for your own design, sent out to at least two or three builders. This should be as comprehensive as possible, down to how many internal doors you need, what kind of flooring you require, what finishes you want on the walls, etc, so spend a lot of time on this. You want to know as accurately as possible how much the house will cost. Remember, if you change your mind about details from this point on, it may cost you extra.

Find builders by asking for recommendations, go to see them where they are currently working, ask to see a selection of houses they have already built. The builders will return the contract with the final price and a start and finish time, and you can choose which one to go with. When you sign the building contract it should list a detailed description of the property to be built, the quantity and quality of the materials to be used and the price for each item, the schedule of construction work and a penalty clause in the event of a late completion. You can agree between yourselves a schedule of payments in stages. Make it clear that any unforeseen costs outside this contract will have to be agreed in advance with you.

You will want to visit the construction site as often as possible to check that all is well. Since you may not be able to be there every day your architect or *geometra* should perform this function for you as part of his duties. The Italians describe this as being *'l'occhio del padrone'* – the eye of the boss. Certainly he should be there every day at the beginning of the project and at all the important points of construction.

Buying from a developer

Check out the developer's credentials – they should be registered at the local Chamber of Commerce. Ask around and find out if the building company is well known in the area and what kind of reputation it has. Go and see other properties that have been built by the same developer. Most new properties are sold prior to the building actually being finished so you may only be able to look at a show house or apartment. This is quite risky in Italy since it may be a year or two years before you can actually get the keys to the finished product. It is much better if you find a property that is nearly finished.

Have the contract checked by a lawyer or *notaio*. You must make sure that you have a firm price for your property and that you will not be asked to pay more money if the developer suddenly comes up against extra costs. You need to have an assurance that the developer has enough money to finish the job and that he is properly insured. Also, if a developer goes out of business and leaves a lot of debt you could be liable to something called *coinvolti,* having to pay a share of the debt according to the deposit you have paid. Sounds mad, I know, but this is Italy. A legal adviser will keep you right, so do not think of buying a new property without consulting one.

If you are buying a property in a residential complex in a coastal resort, you may be offered a property in a later phase of development so at least you can see what has already gone up. Look at the communal swimming pool, sporting and leisure facilities and try to gauge if they are sufficiently large for the numbers of people who will eventually live there. Often these facilities become so overcrowded that they are practically useless. If you can, try to rent a similar property on the site for a couple of days or a week. You may find that it is too noisy for you, too far from the sea or not suitable in other ways. Ask for a written note of the amount of shared service or condominium charges that you will have to pay. Is heating and lighting included or does everyone pay their own bill? What about insurance of the common parts and salaries of the administration staff? If the complex is a few years old, ask for condominium records for the previous years and the minutes of any residency association. Try to speak to someone who is already living there and ask what good and bad points they have to make about the property. Are you free to rent or re-sell your property when you want? Could you work from your property if you want to? Is the place child-friendly? Can you keep pets? Can you park your car? Be tough in negotiating the price – agents in these kinds of properties have a lot of apartments to get off their hands and you should push hard for a discount or an upgrade in the finishing touches. You may be able to negotiate a free parking space, for example.

At the sales office, there will probably be someone who speaks your language, and indeed the contract may be written in English as well as Italian, but have a lawyer examine the paperwork. Buying a new house in Italy is actually more complicated than buying an old one to restore, so you need this reassurance. You will have to pay a deposit of 2 to 10 per cent and then embark on a payment schedule. Find out if you are committed to the sale as soon as you put down your deposit or if there is a cooling-off period during which you can change your mind and have your deposit returned.

Building guarantees

Builders in Italy must give guarantees for their work but your success in claiming compensation if something does go wrong depends on the type of builder you employ and if he is local or not. I would not consider constructing a new house or buying from a developer unless I was convinced that he was financially sound. That means going for a building company of a certain size that has already successfully built properties in the area – not a one- or two-man band, however likeable and trustworthy they seem. If you go for a building team from hundreds of miles away, will you be able to track them down in the future? As with the restoration of an old farmhouse, you have a certain amount of protection if things go wrong. Roughly speaking, if *piccoli danni* (small defects) emerge in the first two years after construction, your builder should return to correct them. If *grandi danni* (large defects) emerge within 10 years, he should do the same. In your building contract, it would be a good idea to specify that you want to hold back 10 per cent of the residual costs for, say, six months so that you can ensure the work has been done to your satisfaction. You must agree this with your builder in advance, however.

 **Utilities**

Electricity

Electricity in Italy is supplied by *Ente Nazionale per L'Energia Elettrica*, the national electricity board that is commonly known as ENEL. It is responsible for bringing the electrical supply to your home, reading meters and increasing or decreasing your power supply. You will find your local office in the telephone directory under ENEL or you can call the freephone service (*servizio clienti numero verde*) 800 900800. As a new client you will have to sign a service contract and will need the following documents: a *codice fiscale*, your passport and a copy of the last meter reading. If you are resident in Italy, you will be entitled to lower rates on your contract than a non-resident. You can go to the local ENEL office on your own to sign the new contract (*voltura delle utenze*) or your estate agent should be able to arrange for the utilities to be transferred to your name from the previous owner. Ask him to verify that all bills from the previous owner have been paid and make sure he does not try to charge you extra for this service – he has already been paid enough! If you are connecting a new supply of electricity to your restored home, your *geometra* should take care of all the paperwork.

Electricity in Italy is expensive, among the most costly in Europe, and a lot of it is imported from France. Therefore Italians regard electricity as a precious resource and they ration it. Instead of having an unlimited supply of power to your house – and paying bills according to how much you have used – you must decide how much power you need. You can start off at 3kwh or 4.5kwh (kilo watt hours) – which is not a lot. It means that when you have some lights on and the television and dishwasher going at the same time, the whole house will plunge into darkness if your teenage daughter decides to use her hairdryer. You have gone over your allotted supply and the electricity trip switch will shut off the power.

This is alarming the first time it happens but you soon get used to it. You shut down some of the appliances that caused the trouble in the first place, flick the trip switch back and the electricity comes on again. But it is very annoying and so most people go for 6kwh or 10kwh – this means that you can run several high-energy appliances at once. If you have guests or renters to stay, tell them that there is a limited power supply to all Italian houses and that they cannot leave all the lights blazing. Keep torches handy and make it clear where the trip switch is (usually outside in the garden) so that if the power does trip, everyone knows how to switch it on again. Make full use of timers for irrigation systems – have them come on in the middle of the night – so that they do not overload the electricity supply just when you are cooking dinner.

Bills are issued every two months and are calculated on your estimated consumption rather than the actual one. Unlike France, there are no special packages with different pricing structures, depending on your consumption of electricity. You will pay a subscription charge and the rest of the bill is dependent on the level of your power supply. As you go up the kwh scale, you pay more per unit. A bill based on your real consumption, known as a *conguaglio*, is issued yearly and if you have overpaid a refund will be sent which you can cash at a post office. You can pay your ENEL bills at banks, electricity offices or post offices but it is best to have utilities paid by direct debit, especially if you are not always in the country. If bills are left unpaid you may be cut off without warning and it will be expensive and time-consuming to be reconnected.

The electricity supply in Italy is 220 volts 50Hz, so many electrical appliances from the UK will work here. You will simply have to change to Italian plugs, which are un-fused and have two or three prongs in a single row.

You can pay for unsightly electricity poles to be re-sited further from your house or buried underground. We had an electricity pole right in front of our farmhouse and were able, after waiting only a few months, to have it moved out of sight, opening up our view. The problem is that you cannot apply to have this done until you actually own the house so there is a bit of a risk involved. A *geometra* should be able to give you an indication of whether or not you will be allowed to move an electricity (or telephone) pole. Sadly, this does not apply to the huge, ghastly electricity pylons that blot the Italian landscape.

Gas

If you are living in a rural area of Italy you will probably have to have a *bombolone* (gas tank) installed that can be topped up regularly from a tanker. The gas supplier you choose, such as Ecogas, will arrange for its safe installation. It has to be at least 7 metres from the house, well away from any trees, and will be buried underground. Your *geometra* can help out with the paperwork for this since the local fire department has to be informed of its location on your property. Tanks come in various sizes, depending on the size of the house, but the most common tank holds around 1,000 litres of liquid gas. Most companies offer a 20 per cent discount in September if you want to fill your tank for winter. This is an expensive method for heating and hot water but it is efficient. In winter, for example, we pay approximately 300 euros a month for heating our four bedroom house, despite having a log fire.

If you are living in or next to a big city or town you will be connected to the mains gas supplied by *Societa Italiana per il Gas* (ITALGAS or SIG). You will need to have the name on the meter transferred from the previous owners to you. You will have to sign a service contract and will need the same identification as for the electricity contract. Your bill will also come every two months and will be an estimated one, with a refund for over-payment (*conguaglio*) yearly.

Some Italians use bottled gas for cooking. You pay a deposit on the first bottle and then exchange empty ones for full ones. They can be purchased in supermarkets, garages or delivered to your home. Propane gas is recommended, rather than butane, for internal use.

Other heating methods

Wood-burning stoves are used in many Italian homes and a small one costs upwards of 500 euros. But these are suitable only for heating a single room. A wood-fuelled boiler system will cost 2,000 euros upwards – many of my friends have them – and their houses are very toasty! If you live in a small house in the country, this is an option well worth considering, but you will have to have suitable outside storage for large amounts of wood. You can gather the wood yourself or buy it – through the first months of winter many Italians set up small woodcutting businesses. A *quintale* of wood is 100kg and each *quintale* will cost between 12 and 20 euros, depending on which part of Italy you live in. This does not include the cost of stacking the wood: you would have to pay extra or do it yourself. You can gather your own firewood – a very satisfying thing to do. If you have quite a bit of land you should cut down dead trees and make use of them. However, if you want to cut down big trees on your land you must consult the *Guardia Forestale*, whose number you will find in the telephone book. Tell them you want to cut down some trees and ask if they will make a visit. This service is free and they will tell you which trees can go and which must remain. Their duty is to protect the countryside so that beautiful old trees are preserved for future generations.

Electricity is used to heat small apartments or houses because it is easy and inexpensive to install, but running costs are very high. You should not under any circumstances consider putting electric radiators into a large house. The radiators are unsightly and they will be inefficient for heating large areas. Invest in a proper central heating system!

Sansa is a by-product of the olive oil pressing process. Once the oil has been extracted from the olives, the kernels are dried. The resulting fuel is highly calorific and creates very little ash. Although it can be purchased in log form, more usually it is sold loose and has the appearance of chopped nuts. It is used in a specially designed boiler and can provide both heating and hot water. It is one of the most economical methods of heating a home in Italy and in November and December, during the olive harvest, you will see *sansa* being loaded from the *frantoios* (olive oil mills) onto tractors or trailers to go to heat farmers' houses. If you are thinking about this method of heating you must make sure you have regular, dependable deliveries and a large storage area near your boiler. Running out of *sansa* in the midst of an Italian winter can be most unpleasant.

Under-floor heating is becoming very popular in Italy because it negates the need for unsightly radiators and it is also cheaper to run. Warm water circulates around pipes embedded into concrete below the terracotta floors. The water can be heated by gas, electricity or oil. A proficient central heating engineer will be able to tell you if your house is suitable for under-floor heating and how much it will cost.

Solar heating is gaining in popularity in Italy, and the government is now offering grants for installing solar panels. However, you may need a back-up heating system for winter.

Water

If you are living in a town you will be connected to the mains. In the country, you may have to depend on a well for your water supply. Most houses will already have their own established *pozzo* (well) or you can ask a water diviner or geologist to come and survey your land with a view to drilling for a new one.

Lack of water can be a serious problem in Italy during the summer, therefore properties with ample supplies of water are much envied. We have our own *pozzo* that has always given us masses of water until last year when four months without rain lowered the water table in our part of Umbria so much that the *pozzo* was unable to cope. I came home one afternoon to find it spluttering air, indicating that there was insufficient water to draw out. *'Siamo rovinati!'* (We are ruined!') said Filippo, who helps us in the garden. We had to resort to buying water by the tanker load – at 60 euros a time – to keep the garden watered. It was an expensive and worrying summer. Our well did recover but the water came back slowly and we had to ration it for weeks afterwards. We have never taken our water supply for granted again.

Use all means at your disposal to conserve water, especially if you live in the countryside. You can have a plastic storage tank installed in an outbuilding that is topped up automatically when the level lowers with use. Ours has a capacity of 500 litres and it means that we have enough water for showers and cooking for several days if the *pozzo* plays up. Because this water source is near the house, we also have much better pressure in our showers. In addition, we have an old underground water cistern that stores water for the garden with rainfall and the automatic topping up system.

If you are buying a property with a well or a *sorgente* (spring) on the land, verify if anyone else has the right to use it. Often, wells and springs are shared among neighbours. This system usually works well but can lead to trouble during drought when a farmer might naturally think he has more call on the water than you. You may also want to have the water analysed to check that it is safe to drink.

If you are restoring a property and are near a town or village, you can pay to be connected to the mains supply but you will have to pay for the excavation and digging work involved and the laying of the pipes. Your *geometra* can provide you with an estimated price for the work and do the necessary paperwork. If you are living in a town or city, the water company will either install a meter or calculate your bill depending on the size of your house or apartment.

Telephone

The national telephone company SIP (*Società Italiana per L'Esercizio delle Telecommunicazioni*) was privatized in 1997 and is now known as Telecom Italia. Services are much more efficient and you do not have to wait months to have a new telephone installed, as used to be the case. ISDN lines are available all over Italy but ADSL lines are currently restricted to major towns and cities and are being slowly rolled out. To check ADSL availability in your part of Italy using your local dialling code, go to www.tin.virgilio.it and type in ADSL in the *prodotti servizi* section. Telecom Italia did have a monopoly on all fixed-phone lines but in the past couple of years companies such as Tiscali, Infostrada, Teledue and Wind have introduced much-needed competition and brought down prices accordingly.

As the owner of a new home in Italy, you will need either a *subentro* (taking over an existing telephone) or a *nuovo impianto* (new installation). You can ask your estate agent to help you with a *subentro* or ask your *geometra* to do the necessary request and paperwork for a new telephone line. If your Italian is good enough you can do this yourself and go directly to a Telecom Italia office or speak to them by dialling 182. Telecom Italia will write to tell you what your new telephone number will be and the date on which engineers will arrive to install the new equipment. The waiting time is approximately two weeks but will vary according to which part of Italy you live in.

Telephone bills are sent every two months; again, if you have a holiday home it would be best to put these payments on direct debit so that you are not inadvertently cut off. Homeowners pay a rental charge and tax, and then the rest of the bill is calculated on the number of *scatti* (telephone points) that you use. You should investigate the other telephone providers to see if you can get a better deal than with Telecom Italia. In this way you pay the rental line charge and taxes to Telecom Italia but make your calls through another company.

For example, with Telecom Italia you pay 30.98 *centesime* as soon as your call to London is answered. After that, it costs 19.36 *centesime* a minute. With the provider Tiscali it is considerably cheaper – 15.49 *centesime* on reply and 12.50 *centesime* every minute thereafter. Register for this service at www.tiscali.it (look for the word *recaricasa*) and you will have to pay a certain amount in advance, for example, 50 euros. Before every call you dial 10030, then the number. If you want to know how much credit remains on your account you can sign on to the Web site or dial 800 0091. The provider Teledue has a similar system – you dial a prefix before every number – although you can request a box that sits on your telephone table and negates the need for the pre-dialled code. On the Tiscali Web site you can see comparative tariffs for international calls for all the Italian providers.

Once your landline is installed your name will automatically go into the local telephone directory and you will find yourself targeted by marketing companies that want to sell you something or ask for your views in a survey. This happens to me at least twice a week and I use these calls as a free Italian lesson, telling the person on the other end of the line that I am learning Italian and that if they want to talk to me they will have to speak very slowly. They are usually delighted to do so and I have learnt a lot of new vocabulary this way, so don't put the phone down when these people call – make use of the chance to talk in Italian.

There are five mobile phone networks in Italy – Omnitel, TIM, Wind, G and Blu. When deciding which company to sign up with, check that its network includes your home area, since cover can be patchy; for example, the Wind service does not operate fully in Marche. You can get good advice – and most of the assistants will speak some English – in the mobile phone shops that are in every Italian town. If you are unsure about which contract to sign, start off with a pay-as-you-go phone, topping up the charges with pre-paid cards.

To call Directory Enquiries, dial 12. It is a fully automated system – you do not speak to a human operator – and therefore quite difficult to use if your Italian is not good. You can ask for only one telephone number per call.

Settling in

Learn the language

You make many mistakes when learning a new language. While looking for our house in Italy, I was in touch with an *agente immobiliare* called Paolo, whom I had met on previous house-hunting trips. I was puzzled when his e-mails became rather flirtatious, addressing me as *carissima* Barbara and suggesting he take me out for dinner the next time I was in his area. I couldn't understand this sudden over-familiarity until I discovered I had been writing to him in the familiar second person singular rather than the formal third person singular that you should use for business correspondence. I had also been writing, 'I can't wait to see you again' at the end of all my messages when I thought that I was merely saying that I looked forward to our next meeting. No wonder poor old Paolo had a gleam in his eye – he thought I was looking for a *storia d'amore* as well as a house to buy.

Learning a new language when you are an adult is hard work but it is surprising how many people contemplate buying a property in Italy without even trying to pick up the basics. It is true that in places like Rome, Milan or Florence you can live in almost totally English-speaking environments, but what is the fun of that? You will always be an outsider if you don't learn the language. You will be missing out if you are not able to have a conversation with your Italian neighbours, read the local news-papers or socialize at dinner parties. You are making a huge financial investment by buying property in Italy and it is madness to be unable to communicate properly. Quite apart from the cultural aspect of it, think what would happen in emergency situations – like a fire, a burst pipe, or a road accident – and you were unable to make yourself understood.

Admittedly, it is a tall order to learn a new language but nobody expects you to become fluent overnight. Simple chores that we take for granted in our home country, like dealing with the bank or the post office, will be intimidating at first. For me, going to the cheese and cold meats counter at my local co-op, where you have to shout out your order as half a dozen impatient Italian housewives wait their turn, used to be a major ordeal. I would go into the shop thinking that I must get two or three different kinds of *pecorino*, ask which *mozzarella* they recommend and find out what is the best local *prosciutto*. But when my ticket number was called, my mind would go blank and I would end up ordering something simple like a roast chicken, instead of what I really wanted. Being fazed like this is all part of this adventure – it does get easier – and you just have to get on with it! Imagine how irritated you would be if you met someone living in your own country who refused to learn your language.

Men are the worst culprits when it comes to learning. Time and time again, I meet foreign couples where the wife speaks passable Italian and the husband can string only a few sentences together. Men seem frightened of failure, or of making fools of themselves, so they find excuses not to learn. The result is that men depend on their wives to be translators, which is tiring for her and frustrating for him. I went to language classes to learn Italian but my husband has been picking it up as he goes along, which is a lot harder.

One day I picked up the telephone at home and my husband shouted down the line: 'Fool! Fool!' Naturally, I asked what on earth he was talking about. He was at a garage getting petrol, had forgotten the word for 'full' and was becoming progressively more flustered as he tried to tell the attendant that he wanted a full tank of petrol. In restaurants and bars because he hadn't learnt any verbs, he would bark his request: 'The bill!' or 'A double espresso!' When it was pointed out that it sounded rude and that he should talk in a sentence, he went completely the other way and was tortuously well-mannered: 'Excuse me, please, thank you very much, may I have a coffee, please, thank you very much.' My husband also learnt some of his Italian through conversations with our 80-year-old gardener Filippo until English friends who have lived in Tuscany for many years pointed out that he was speaking in dialect, had picked up Filippo's accent and sounded like the Italian equivalent of Bert Grundy from 'The Archers'.

One of the times when you will wish you spoke the language fluently is when you are dealing with Italian workmen. Every foreigner is driven to distraction by the inability of Italian plumbers, painters or electricians to finish a job or even to turn up at all. It is very frustrating if you can only talk in a couple of tortured phrases to some recalcitrant builder. He is hardly likely to take you seriously when you have the conversational level of a six-year-old.

I inadvertently hit on an answer to this problem early on in our life in Italy when some workmen let me down. I had been waiting weeks for them to finish a few small jobs in the house and eventually two of them turned up and promised they would finish all the outstanding work. They were young, good-looking Italian boys with sunglasses, shirts unbuttoned to their navels and cigarettes permanently dangling from their lips. They looked like something out of a Bertolucci film as they swaggered around the place. The morning went well, off they went for lunch and I assumed they would be back in the afternoon. No one turned up. I was furious and I couldn't contact them because their mobile phones were switched off. They pitched up the next day, with some lame excuse that one of them had felt unwell because of a cold. What had really happened was that they had arranged another job elsewhere and had just left me in the lurch. I wanted to say: 'You can't pull the wool over my eyes. I don't believe your story for a second. Why didn't you telephone me? Don't think I'm some foreigner you can take advantage of ... blah de blah ....' But all I could splutter was... 'Me angry woman. Me ... not pay bill.' It was so frustrating that I let rip in English. I knew they couldn't understand a word of what I was saying but they got the general drift that I was mad as hell. My outburst had the desired effect and they worked until the job was done, although I'm sure they thought I was some hysterical old nutcase. I have since found it useful, if you really do have a reason to be angry with workmen, to be a bit dramatic in your own language. Don't overdo it, but they will understand from the tone of your voice that you are not happy and it will do you good to let off steam!

The best way to learn Italian is to go to an organized class. I have been to several language courses in the last few years and when you are stumbling over tenses or vocabulary it's good to know that other people have the same problems. It is by far the best way of learning and much more fun because you are all in it together. When you are out and about in Italy, preface whatever you are going to say with: *sto imperando italiano* (I am learning Italian). Most people will be patient and will help and encourage you. When you get the chance to have a conversation with an Italian, don't be embarrassed if they correct you – it's one of the best ways to learn. Once you have bought your house, and especially if you are re-building, have a list of essential words on hand that you can refer to and try to learn them off by heart. A little bit of studying will make you feel much more confident. There is some useful vocabulary at the back of the book to help you.

There is a range of resources – language courses, CDs, tapes and books – to assist you in learning Italian. Most local authorities in the UK offer part-time language courses – see your local authority's Web site for details or ask for information in your local library. *Floodlight* is the official guide to part-time and full-time courses run by government-funded colleges, universities and adult education centres in all the London boroughs. See www.floodlight.co.uk.com.

The Italian Cultural Institute, 39 Belgrave Square, London, has a range of intensive and part-time language courses. See www.italcultur.org.uk for more details, or phone 0207 235 1461. This is where I learnt my Italian and I absolutely loved it, even the masses of homework that they give you to do.

There are hundreds of language schools all over Italy for foreigners. It is a terrific way to spend a holiday while soaking up the culture of the country. Below is a list of a few schools; you can find others at www.it-schools.com:

- Bologna – Centro Culture Italiana, Via Castiglione 4, Bologna, Tel: 051–228003. Societa Dante Aligheri, Via Pignattari 1, Bologna, Tel: 051–226658
- Milan – Berlitz, Via Larga 8, Milan, Tel: 02–8690814. Lingua Due, Corso Buenos Aires 43, Milan, Tel: 02295 19972
- Rome – Instituto Italiano, Via Merulana 139, Rome, Tel: 06–70452138. Scuola Leonardo da Vinci, Corso Vittorio Emanuele 39, Rome, Tel: 06–70452138
- Florence – British Institute of Florence, Palazzo Strozzino, Piazza Strozzi, Florence, Tel: 055 2677 8200, Web site www. britishinstitute.it. Scuola Lorenzo de Medici, Via Faenza 43, Florence, Tel: 055287 360
- Naples – L'Italiano Centro di Lingua e Cultura, Vico Santa Maria dell'Aiuto 17, Naples, Tel: 081 552 4331

The BBC *Italianissimo* language course is very useful to study by yourself at home. See www.bbc.co.uk for information. I found the BBC's Italian grammar book by Alwena Lamping to be one of the best reference books around, a bargain buy at £5.99.

Retiring to Italy

Many people buy a home in Italy with a view to retiring there. Better weather, a more relaxed way of life and lower living costs make the country an attractive retirement prospect. Older people are treated with great respect in Italy and foreign retirees can fit very well into a small, thriving community. Retiring to Italy is not a decision to make lightly, of course, and most of the people who decide to do so will already know what kind of lifestyle to expect. You will have had a holiday home here for some time, be familiar with your particular area and have some expertise in speaking Italian. If this is not the case, it would be better to rent a house or an apartment before doing anything drastic such as selling your prime residence back home.

Retired expatriates do not need to worry about losing contact with their families when they move to Italy – budget air travel means children and grandchildren can easily visit – and you will be very popular if you can provide a cheap holiday destination. But you do need to think about what would happen if you become ill or lose a partner. Unless you have built up a very good support network of friends, living in Italy under such circumstances could be very difficult. Elsewhere in the book I have warned against choosing somewhere too quiet to live or too isolated in terms of transport. It is worth repeating that pensioners need other people around them, they need familiar things as points of reference and they need to feel that they belong.

You will have no problems receiving state or private pensions in Italy. You will simply have to make arrangements for the money to be trans- ferred to your bank account in Italy or to leave it in your home country and withdraw the money from there. There may be slight fluctuations in value because of the euro, but a bank manager or private financial adviser will give advice on the most economical way to set this up.

As a retiree you are also entitled to use the Italian health service in the same way as an Italian pensioner would do.

Driving and buying a car

Driving in Italy is an interesting experience. Charming, mild-mannered Italians turn into aggressive maniacs as soon as they take to the roads and we sensible foreigners are left stupefied by the risks they take. Overtaking on a blind curve, reversing on a motorway, tailgating, ignoring red lights – Italian driving offences are numerous. Apparently you can buy a sweater in Naples with a black stripe painted diagonally on it. You wear it while driving; it looks from a distance like you are wearing a seatbelt and you can screech around Naples at high speed, unencumbered by something that might save your life in a high-speed crash. Very macho. My *geometra* told me this while we were reversing – the wrong way, of course – down the narrow, medieval streets of Orvieto. He thought it was hilarious.

Italians have the highest numbers of cars per head of any country in Europe – 600 for every 1,000 inhabitants. They are addicted to watching *Formula Uno* and it has been suggested that this is why national driving skills are so appalling. Every man thinks he is Michael Schumacher even if he is driving a one-litre, diesel-engined Opel Corsa. Bad driving applies mainly to male drivers, but some Italian women are just as dangerous. One of my neighbours drives in the middle of the road, takes blind bends at breakneck speed and doesn't seem terribly concerned about keeping her eyes on the road at all times, preferring to look at the person she is talking to. I am a bag of nerves when I accept a lift from her.

The Italian government has recognized that it needs to do more to create a road safety culture, therefore prevention, enforcement and sanctions are now the order of the day and it is making a difference in terms of lowering the fatality rate, which is some 6,000 deaths a year. Maximum driving speeds are 130 kph on *autostrade* and 110 kph to 90 kph on lesser main roads.

Patente a punti (driving licence with points) was introduced in 2003 and this system penalizes violations of the Highway Code. Everyone has 20 points on their driving licence and points are deducted for bad driving. Lose too many points and you could be fined, made to sit a driving theory test or have your licence confiscated. However, the list of punishable violations, compiled from the past sins of Italian drivers, shows what the government is up against. You can lose points for: driving on the wrong side of the road at a curve or in low visibility, reversing on the motorway, not using indicators, driving too fast in a tunnel, failing to stop at a road block, failing to stop at red lights, using a mobile phone without earphones, going the wrong way up a one-way street, etc. Italian police also have road campaigns at various times during the year when they can double the penalty points for driving too fast or using a mobile phone.

It is now law in Italy that headlights be switched on when driving on all roads, even in the daytime. If you are caught not wearing a seatbelt you may be cautioned or fined. If you are caught twice in 12 months not wearing a seatbelt you may lose your licence to drive for a year. The macho drivers in Naples may find their days are numbered.

If you are bringing a car into Italy on a temporary basis you can drive it on foreign number plates for a year if you are a non-resident, provided you have an international driving licence. If you are a resident, you must apply for it to be properly registered. Your car must pass an inspection test and this is where Italian bureaucracy rears its ugly head again. The rules for the inspection change constantly, but the car has to pass certain tests for engine size, tyre size, emissions, etc. This proves particularly difficult for American cars and it is generally not financially beneficial and too much trouble to import an ordinary American car to Italy. Owners of all cars from outside Italy may be asked to make modifications to comply with Italian environmental standards – so check the technical data with your manufac- turer before thinking about having your car registered in Italy.

Only residents with a *codice fiscale* can buy cars in Italy. New cars are expensive because of high taxes but you can pick up a good second-hand car through a garage or through adverts in your local newspaper. If you buy a used car privately you must pay a fee to transfer ownership. The licence plates – *targa nazionale* – stay with the car. You will also pay road tax, depending on the size of the engine and what fuel the car runs on. Make sure the previous owner has paid outstanding road tax. If he or she hasn't, the bill will be transferred to you as the new owner.

Insurance

Insurance is usually third-party cover only, which covers the car and not the driver and insures you for the cost of damage and injury in accidents for which you are to blame. You can also add collision cover that pays for damage to your car in the event of an accident for which you are respon- sible. Comprehensive cover is generally regarded as too expensive but you can ask an insurance company to give you a quote that will encompass all the liabilities you would normally have with compre- hensive cover in your own country, and see how much it costs. Most Italians favour the *bonus malus* (no claims) type of cover where the premium you pay depends on how accident-prone you have been.

Two insurance companies operating in Italy – AXA and SARA – offer cheaper third-party insurance for infrequent drivers. This may suit people with holiday homes who drive for short periods in Italy. Details are available from the companies or from the ACI (Italian Automobile Club). Another insurance company called RAS offers a weekend and holiday policy that may also be useful to foreigners. The *patente a punti* system applies to non-Italian residents who buy cars and theoretically it also applies to foreigners driving their own cars.

If you are not an Italian resident, and not from a country within the EU, but want to buy a car, you can go to your *commune* and ask for an *atto sostitutivo*. You do not have to pay a registration tax for the first year and will be given foreigners' licence plates (*escursionisti esteri*). After 12 months you will either have to sell the car or take it out of the country, which means that you will have to pay the tax. If you are from an EU country you can drive to and from Italy in your own car with your own insurance, but you need to check with your insurance company as to how long you are covered for a single visit to Italy. In some cases there may be an extra charge. All of this is complicated and time-consuming and you may want to pay a specialist agent to sort out the paperwork relating to cars and driving licences – you will find agents in the Italian Yellow Pages under *pratiche automobilistiche*.

Members of an EU country can keep their driving licences while in Italy. Non-EU citizens should check if their home country has a reciprocity agreement with Italy – they may be required to take an Italian driving test. An Italian driving licence is renewable every 10 years until the age of 55, and every 5 years thereafter. Over the age of 70 a medical certificate from your doctor may be required to say that you are in good health and fit to drive.

Driving rules

A general reminder: driving in Italy is on the right and speed limits are 130 kph on the *autostrade*. Italy is criss-crossed with a network of *autostrade* (toll-highways). When you enter an *autostrade* you are issued with a ticket and you return the ticket and pay a toll when you exit. There are also *superstrade* (free expressways).

Red tape

Italy is one of the most bureaucratic countries in the world and there is a certain amount of documentation needed to stay in Italy. Obtaining these documents can be a time-consuming process that often involves several visits to the relevant offices. If you don't have time or don't want to do it yourself there are agencies that you can pay to do the work on your behalf. You can find them under *Agenzie Certificati* in the Italian Yellow Pages or under Relocation Services in the English version of Yellow Pages.

Visas

Citizens of the EU, the USA and Canada do not require a visa to enter Italy for a stay of up to 90 days. Other foreign nationals should consult the Italian Embassy or Consulate in their home country to find out entry qualifications. This must be done prior to arrival in Italy.

Permesso di soggiorno

Any visitor intending to stay in Italy for longer than three months is required to register at the local police headquarters (*questura*) within eight days of arrival and to apply for a *permesso di soggiorno*. This means that you are permitted to live in Italy but not that you are resident there. You must go to the *questura*, ask for the appropriate form and return with: your passport; the completed *permesso* application; three passport-sized photographs, and a *marca da bollo* (see below). If you do not have a job in Italy you must provide proof that you have means of supporting yourself during your stay – showing credit cards will usually suffice. You may also be required to show that you have some form of private medical insurance. The time allotment of your *permesso* depends on the purpose of your stay – eg if you are a student, retiree, property owner. If you are an EU national, you will receive a *permesso* for five years. If you come from outside the EU, it may only be valid for a year. Students who wish to stay and study in Italy must bring all the above documents and certificate of enrolment in a university to the *questura*. It may take up to 30 days for your *permesso* to arrive.

Marca da bollo

This is the tax stamp used for official documents. These can be bought in a *tabaccherie* (tobacco shop). *Carta bollata* is official paper that already has the tax stamp on it and can also be bought in a *tabaccherie*. These are required for non-EU citizens.

Codice fiscale

This is an individual tax number, similar to the British National Insurance number or the US Social Security number. It is one of the easiest documents to obtain and you must have it to open a bank account, buy property, be paid by an employer, buy a car, etc. Go to the *Ufficio delle Imposte Dirette* (local tax office) or *Ufficio Anagrafe* (local registry office) with your passport and you will be given one immediately. The reason the authorities are so accommodating with this piece of red tape is that they can now collect taxes from you!

Residency

If you plan to spend more than 183 days a year in Italy, you must apply for residency. This will make life easier for you – utilities bills will cost half as much as a non-resident pays, for example. You will be able to buy and register a car and open a bank account, instead of being limited to the accounts for *stranieri* (foreigners). To obtain residency go to the *Ufficio Anagrafe* at your local *comune* and simply apply. You will need your passport, *permesso di soggiorno* and three passport-sized photographs. You will be asked how many are in your family – eg if you are single, married, have children – so that this can be noted for local census purposes. If you are already known within your community you can probably have your residency certificate very quickly – I got mine on the same day. Other *comunes* will take longer and may even send the *vigile urbano* (local civil police) to check that you are, indeed, living full-time at the address you put on the form. A residence permit for an EU national is usually valid for five years. For non-EU nationals it will only be for one year. There is a fee for the paperwork involved, approximately 5 to 10 euros.

Citizenship

It is possible to obtain Italian citizenship, or dual citizenship, if:

- you were born in Italy and are over 21 years old;
- one of your parents is Italian;
- you are married to an Italian citizen for 3 years or more;
- you have been living legally in Italy for 10 years.

House insurance

Once you have bought your house, even if it in the process of being restored, you should insure it against fire, damage and public liability. Don't make my mistake – I bought an Italian insurance policy without realizing I was signing up for the next 10 years. The contract was in Italian so, of course, I couldn't read it all the way through and just assumed I was signing up for a year. I discovered the error the following summer when our house had been restored and I needed a more comprehensive policy that included contents insurance. Apparently it is quite normal to be committed to an insurance policy for 10 years but no one, including the insurance agent, had told me this fact. I have had to pay both premiums this year – luckily the first premium is for only a small amount – and I will be able to cancel it next year by giving six months' written notice. But it serves me right for not checking more thoroughly... you have been warned!

When taking out an insurance policy you will be asked what kind of security arrangements are in place at your house since this will determine the cost of your policy. Do you have a burglar alarm? Are there bars on the windows and doors? Do you have shutters? Is the house left unoccupied? Tell your insurance company if you intend to let out your property – this is very important as you need tenant liability cover.

Get professional advice from your *geometra* or architect on the cost of a complete re-build in the event of fire or other disaster. Don't be tempted to under-insure either for re-building or against theft. It is a false economy and you will regret it. Note that it is not possible to insure your house against earthquake damage. In the past the Italian government has paid for re-building properties after an earthquake, assessing the value of the house based on what appears on the land registry, plus a small amount for inflation. After the last earthquake in Marche in 1996, for example, the government phased the payments so that only people with sole residences, ie people who lived there full-time, got re-building grants fairly quickly. Everyone else, ie second-home owners, had payments phased over five years.

Grants are distributed region by region and in tranches, so you may have to wait for compensation. At the time of writing it has been suggested that the Italian government wants to introduce earthquake insurance – homeowners will have to pay for their own cover. This could come into force in the next few years.

Most large towns have insurance companies where someone speaks a bit of English – the expatriate grapevine will probably have some recommendations. Alternatively, you may want to consider using a UK insurer – the policy will be in English, any claim can be made in English and you may feel happier with this. Andrew Copeland International Ltd specializes in Italian insurance. Their policy also covers clients for emergency travel to Italy to sort out a claim, if necessary. Tel: 0181 656 2544.

Television and radio

For me, *la dolce vita* means listening to the 'Today' programme or 'The Archers' while sitting in the sunshine in our garden. With a cup of coffee, a comfortable chair and a view of vineyards and olive groves, it is bliss to hear John Humphreys bullying another interviewee or hear Kenton Archer and Linda Snell bickering over the latest goings-on in Ambridge.

Along with thousands of other expatriates in Italy, I listen to Radio Four and Radio Two through Sky on channels 854 and 852 respectively. In the summer of 2003 the BBC removed their channels from the encrypted Sky service, causing a wailing and gnashing of teeth all over Italy. This meant that we could no longer receive BBC1, BBC2 or any of the BBC radio stations that had been available as part of Sky. For those of us who want to keep in touch with the news from home, this was a serious blow. The current situation is that Radio 2 and Radio 4 have returned and I have heard that people in the north of Italy who have 1.5 metre satellite dishes are able once again to pick up BBC TV channels, ITV and Channel Four. Those of us in central and south Italy live in hope that the same service will eventually reach here.

You might be appalled that we Brits in Italy are forsaking Italian radio or television. The reason is this: Italy as a country has many cultural delights but its broadcasting services are not among them. Radio stations are filled with semi-hysterical Italian DJs playing sappy pop songs or conducting phone-ins about football, while Italian television is, by and large, mind-numbing drivel. There are a couple of honourable exceptions, decent late-night news programmes like *Porta a Porta* on RAI Uno and the Maurizio Costanza show on Canale 5, but the rest of it is a hotchpotch of game shows, trashy soaps and soft-porn cabaret shows. Despite all this, practically every Italian home has a television and it is often left blaring in the background while families eat lunch. However, there are signs that Italians are tiring of trash TV – an organization called the National Viewers' Union has organized boycotts of television where Italians are encouraged not to watch TV for a single day in protest at the low standards and to take their *telecommandos* (remote controls) to museums and art galleries, where they will receive discounted admission. The last such boycott attracted 300,000 supporters, not a lot in a country of approximately 58 million people, but it's progress!

For the owners of holiday homes, whether to install a television or not can be the subject of considerable debate. Do you really want to watch the Italian version of 'Who Wants To Be A Millionaire' (although it is very useful for learning Italian) on your precious two-week holiday or are you buying a house in Italy so you can return to the tranquil days of reading a book at night, enjoying a conversation, or listening to the crickets outside? In my experience, especially for those who hope to rent out their houses, it is better to have a choice. Indeed some rental agents will not take on a house unless the owner agrees to install satellite TV and a DVD player. Clients expect to be able to plonk their kids in front of the screen while they enjoy a bottle of Chianti in the garden.

Italy has six main TV channels. The three state-owned stations are RAI:

▪ *RAIuno* – the most popular station. It shows films, quiz shows, news and soap operas.

▪ *RAIdue* – made-for-TV films and soaps, such as a dubbed version of 'Friends'.

▪ *RAItre* – more sports-oriented and also contains regional news programmes. For more information see the Web site www.rai.it, which has an English language section.

The other three main TV stations are owned by the Italian Prime Minister Silvio Berlusconi. They are:

I *Canale 5* – films, soaps, news.
I *Italia1* – news and general entertainment programmes.
I *Rete4* – made-for-TV films.

As to be expected, there are no English language channels so many people install a satellite system. To do this you will need to find an *antennista* – you can look them up in the telephone directory.

Some people choose Sky Italia and others opt to register a Sky decoder to a UK address and then transport the box to Italy and connect it to their satellite dish in order to receive Sky channels. Strictly speaking, this is breaching the copyright regulations since Sky only has copyright to broadcast to the UK. You cannot register a Sky box or subscription card to an overseas address. If you are found out, in theory, Sky could block your signal. However, Sky cards are openly sold to expatriates through satellite magazines and expatriate press, albeit at an inflated price. This gives you all the normal channels such as Sky News, Sky One, some movies and sports channels, Paramount, MTV, etc.

There are other packages that enable you to receive English language channels from the Astra and Hot Bird satellites. Hot Bird, for example, carries BBC Prime and BBC World. But the situation relating to Sky may well change again and it is useful to visit the Web site www.satellites.co.uk and go to the discussion forum where you can ask questions about satellite availability in Italy.

A television licence, called a *canone,* costs 99.60 euros and one is required per household, no matter how many televisions you have. The licence fee can be paid at the post office, in some tobacconists, in banks and via the Internet at www.poste.it. Don't be tempted to cheat on your television licence payment since the *carabinieri* have powerful detector vans and fines for non-payment are high. Apparently they use helicopters to sweep mountainous areas, looking for licence dodgers.

Some people want to take their old televisions out to Italy. You will be able to watch television from satellite receivers but you cannot watch Italian terrestrial television, so it is better to buy a television in Italy. You should buy a multi-region DVD player because this will enable you to buy or rent films on DVD in the Italian language, which you can reset to play in English, with Italian sub-titles. When buying a VCR ensure you get one that is multi-system.

Digital terrestrial TV is being introduced and will quadruple the number of channels.

Swimming pools

A swimming pool is a highly desirable addition to your Italian house – an investment that will give you and your family endless hours of fun as well as adding to the value of your property. The swimming pool will be a prominent feature of your home so the site is of paramount importance. Your view to and from the pool and its proximity to the house are crucial… don't have it so close that you are in danger of falling into the water every time you step out of the back door or that it becomes an eyesore in winter when it is unused and covered up. If the pool is too far away, however, you and your guests will find it tiring trudging up and down to the house every time someone wants to go to the loo or have a drink. The pool must also be placed where it can take maximum advantage of available sunlight. This means tracking the daily pattern of the sun on your land, where it rises, how long it stays and when it fades in the afternoon, before choosing the site. Take winds into consideration – your pool should be in a sheltered position. You must also think about issues such as the slope of the site, the type of soil on which the pool will be built and any possible drainage problems. Privacy, boundaries with neighbours and existing plants and trees are other factors.

You can opt for a small, simple pool if you have budgetary or space constraints, or you can create a pool to your own tastes. Square, rectangular, circular or kidney-shaped – the size and shape is down to you. I heard of someone in Umbria who has spent 300,000 euros on their pool. It has waterfalls with real rocks, water slides and a fake beach. Why not, if you've got the money?

You must consult a professional when planning and building your swimming pool. Don't even think about *fai da te* (DIY). Your architect or *geometra* will be able to advise you. They will be familiar with construction methods and materials and can negotiate with and supervise the contractor. Remember that planning permission must be sought from the *comune*. If you are planning a pool on a steep site or in an earthquake zone you may be told to consult a soil or structural engineer.

Once granted, planning permission usually lasts for three years, so it might be worthwhile applying immediately, even if you cannot afford to install a pool straight away. When you are ready to go, the plans will already be in place. If you are doing a full restoration you will probably be advised to include a swimming pool in your application to the *comune* for these same reasons.

The best means of finding a swimming pool contractor is to get a recommendation from the *geometra* or architect and to talk to other pool owners. Most swimming pool company representatives will show you a book of photographs on their preliminary visit, but you can ask to be taken to see a sample selection of pools already built. This is a good idea if you are not sure about the size or shape that you want. It would also be useful to see how other people have paved the areas around their pools, added external lighting and a pergola, etc. Talk to at least two companies and get them to quote for exactly the same pool package. If the estimates come in at roughly the same price, go for the contractor who has the best local reputation rather than the one who shows you impressive photographs. Many swimming pool companies subcontract the work – one group of workers does the excavation, another group will do the reinforced concrete. There is nothing out of the ordinary with this.

Tiling or PVC

It will take approximately two months to build your swimming pool. Obviously, the construction work is best done in spring when the weather is improving and the pool will be finished in time for summer. Some contractors have waiting lists for this crucial time slot, so try to plan ahead. Most people in my part of Italy seem to go for pools lined either with tiling or PVC. Tiling looks much better but it is more expensive and you may have maintenance problems if tiles come adrift. We chose to line our pool with PVC. It is cheaper, you can choose colours from sand to Mediterranean blue, and apparently PVC-lined pools are easier to maintain and there is less chance of a leak. Ours is only a year old so I cannot absolutely guarantee this, but we have a friend who has had a problem-free PVC-lined pool for 10 years. You can also choose to paint the concrete lining of your pool with special water-resistant paints or use a ready-constructed acrylic shell. We went for a salt-based cleaning system, which seems to work very well, but you can also choose chlorine.

Eco pools

Eco pools are basically swimming ponds, with a swimming area lined in plastic and an outer pond filled with plants, a pump and a water skimmer. The plants do the filtration of the pool instead of using chemicals. These pools are more expensive to install but cost less to run in the long term since they do not use chemicals. They do seem to attract more algae than a normal pool, however.

Cost

People will tell you that a modest swimming pool in Italy costs 10,000 to 20,000 euros. In our experience that is nowhere near the true cost. We built a 12 metre by 5 metre pool – which is a medium size – and the basic package (lining, filtration system, pumps and tubing, etc) cost 13,500 euros. On top of that you have the cost of excavation – a swimming pool needs a really, really, big hole. The hole has to be lined with tons of reinforced concrete and then you have to think about paving around the pool to keep dirt out of the water and prevent the garden becoming waterlogged. An external lighting system and a pergola further bump up the cost. You may also want to think about landscaping the garden around the pool. In the end, we paid about 40,000 euros – we expect it to last for at least 15 years!

Safety

Safety features are an important part of your swimming pool plan. If you have small children, or will be visited by families with small children, you should fence in your pool. Have only one entrance gate that can be locked so that children cannot wander in alone. Never let a child of any age swim unsupervised. Don't have too many people at the pool at any one time – a noisy, overcrowded pool can be dangerous because you may not notice that someone is in trouble in the water. If your pool is not deep enough for diving, warn your guests. Use only unbreakable glasses for refreshments served near the pool because broken glass in the water or on the paving is nearly impossible to remove completely. Do not allow people to drink too much alcohol near your pool – alcohol impairs coordination and balance and can lead people to take stupid risks. Do not allow night swimming unless there is sufficient light in and around the pool area. If there is a thunderstorm, get people out of the water quickly. Lightning can be deadly.

Keeping your pool clean

Your swimming pool contractor will explain how to keep your pool clean by testing the PH balance of the water, backwashing the filter, etc. Regular maintenance is essential – you must be able to see the bottom of the pool clearly and the water should not be cloudy. After one month of back-breaking work trying to keep the pool clear of leaves, dead insects and other debris using nets on long poles, we bought a robot to do the job instead. It is dropped into the pool and goes through a six-hour cleaning programme that sucks up all the nasties and even climbs the wall of the pool to clean along the water's edge. It has been worth every penny we paid for it. Be warned however, that a robot looks like a toy and it will attract young children. Do not let them see the robot at work and put it in the pool in the evening so that it cleans during the night.

Wintering

When autumn comes, you will have to cover your pool. The swimming pool contractor can send along a team that puts a wintering solution in the water, takes out the filter so that it cannot be damaged by frost, protects other working parts with plastic and lays out the cover, which is secured with 'sandbags' filled with water. You should not have to do anything to maintain your pool throughout winter.

Pets

Most people who buy properties in the Italian countryside want to keep dogs and cats. There is never any problem in adopting a kitten or a stray cat in an Italian community – people are only too happy to find good homes for them. Ask your neighbours, go to the local pet shop where there are adverts offering cats for free, or keep an eye out at your local market. Families will come with baskets of kittens hoping people will take them away. Some Italians still regard dogs as working animals and if the dogs do not perform satisfactorily, they are thrown out. My neighbours have three dogs, each of which was found abandoned and frightened by the side of the motorway. Another friend, whose husband is a vet, found her dog cowering in a wood in Abruzzo. She and her children spent two days of their holiday coaxing it to come to them and be fed. It was skeletal and timid but is now a much-cherished family pet. Every region in Italy has a dog pound. Look in the Italian *PagineBianche* telephone directory under *Animali Domestici* and you will find the local branch of *Ente Nazionale per la Protezione degli Animali* (National Association for the Protection of Animals). This is the leading animal welfare society in Italy and offers shelter for stray and abused animals and inexpensive pet hospitals in major towns and cities. If dogs are not housed within a certain limit of time, they are put down humanely, so it is worthwhile choosing a dog from here. You can also find unwanted pets in the small ads in local Italian newspapers.

Pet travel

If you are bringing your own pet into Italy, you need to do some work in advance of its arrival. Most animals can enter Italy if they are accompanied by their owner and a certificate of good health issued by a certified vet in the country of origin no more than 30 days before departure. These certificates are available on the Web site www.italyemb.org or can be requested at the closest Italian consulate to your home.

If you want to take a family pet to Italy from the UK, you need to join the Pet Travel Scheme so that you can go back and forth with your animal without it having to be quarantined. This means having your cat or dog microchipped six months before departure, vaccinated against rabies, undergoing a blood test to ensure the vaccine has been effective, and being certified as fit to travel under the 'pet passport' scheme. Two days before departure, you will have to have your animal checked for tapeworm and ticks. The Department for Environment, Food and Rural Affairs (DEFRA) has an informative Web site, www.defra.gov.uk, and a helpline 0870 241710 about this scheme.

Once in Italy, dogs must have an annual rabies injection, be tattooed or microchipped for identification purposes and registered with the *anagrafe canina* (dog bureau). You should check with an Italian vet about vaccinations against other diseases such as distemper and hepatitis. To find a vet in any area of Italy, contact *Associazione Animal Identification,* Tel + 39 0332 236577. The British Embassy Web site www.britishembassy.it also has names and telephone numbers of vets recommended by other pet owners living in Italy.

For information on exporting your animal out of the UK and for factsheets giving advice on travelling with pets from Europe, the USA and Canada or other countries further afield, visit www.defra.gov.uk for updated information. A full list of laboratories approved to do the blood testing to qualify for the Pet Travel Scheme, information on all approved routes and carriers for use when travelling from the UK from qualifying countries and information on tick and tapeworm treatment is also available from the same source.

Education and health

Education

Education in Italy is compulsory and free from the age of six. However, most children in Italy start their education by attending a state or private nursery school from the age of three. The national curriculum is laid down by the *Ministero della Pubblica Istruzione* (Ministry of Public Education). All schools are co-educational. The average number of children in a class is 25. One hour of religious study every week is included in the curriculum, but parents may ask permission for their child to be exempted. The school year starts in mid-September and finishes in mid-June. Classes are held six days a week in the mornings, with homework and outside interests such as sport, art and music being completed in the afternoons, or five full days. The main school holidays are at Christmas and Easter, and three months in the summer; there are no half-term breaks. Children with mild physical or mental handicaps are integrated into main schools wherever possible and are given an assistant or special teacher to help them. If a child lives more than 3 km from a school, transport on school buses can be provided, with parents paying a small fee to cover costs.

Parents who are planning to move to Italy can contact the *Ufficio Scolastico* at the Italian Consulate in London (see Useful Addresses). Staff will advise parents about the Italian education system and how to register their children for an appropriate school. Information on enrolling children at school is also available from each local *commune*.

The state education system is also open and free to non-Italian children. Teaching is a highly respected occupation in Italy but teachers are not well paid so they often moonlight, giving extra lessons for a fee. This may be of particular interest to parents whose children need to learn Italian quickly. The watershed age for a child to learn a foreign language is about 10 or 11; after that age it becomes progressively more difficult.

Children go to elementary school for the first five years, middle school for the next three years and high school for the final five years. Exams are held at the end of every stage and if a child does not meet the required standards, he or she may be sent back to re-sit the whole year. You may notice that young Italians grow up to be confident people, not shy about expressing their opinions. This is because great emphasis is placed on oral exams, and children are made to stand up in class from an early age to be asked their opinions on various subjects. The school system is as follows:

▌ *Asilo nido* or *scuola materna* – for children aged between 3 and 6, a kind of pre-school that is divided into two categories. *Asilo nido*, which literally translates into baby nest, is a crèche where newborn infants and children up to the age of 3 may be left for the day while their parents work. These establishments are run and subsidized by the local *comune*. *Scuola materna* is for children aged between 3 and 6 and takes the traditional nursery school route by encouraging youngsters to learn through play. These establishments are private or run by the local *comune*, therefore fees will vary from region to region.

▌ *Scuola elementare* – primary school for children aged between 6 and 11. Children begin with basic reading, writing and arithmetic and then move on to broader subjects: science, mathematics, history, geography and a foreign language – French or English. Art, music and sports are also on the syllabus. Pupils are regularly assessed on their performance during each year and must pass the exam for a *diploma di licenza elementare* (primary school leaving certificate) in order to move on to the next stage of their education. Most children wear a *grembiulle* — a blue smock – over their clothes.

▌ *Scuola media* – middle school for children aged between 11 and 14. If small villages do not have these schools, pupils will be bussed to the nearest catchment area. Every *comune* with more than 3,000 inhabitants has a *scuola media*. Pupils remain under the continuous assessment system and at the end of the third year sit written and oral exams in all subjects except religion. Successful candidates who achieve a mark of 60 per cent or more receive their *diploma di licenza media* (middle school diploma) and graduate to upper school.

▌ *Scuola superiore* – high school for children aged 14 upwards. Children must decide at this point what subjects they want to specialize in, with an eye to what they want to do when they leave school. Students who plan to go to university will move to one of two types of *liceo* – *classico* where they will study Latin, Greek, philosophy, history of art, etc as well as basic subjects, or *scientifico* where they will take physics, chemistry, biology, etc. These courses last five years. Other children will decide to go to an *istituto* where they do vocational studies in a diverse range of subjects, from architecture and art to carpentry, plumbing or bookkeeping. Because they have to decide their specialist subjects at such a young age it is common for parents to have a big influence on what type of school their children should go to and for the children to decide, after a period of time, that they want to change tack. It is common, therefore, for teenagers to switch subjects or change schools. At the age of 18 or 19 students who have completed five years study and pass *maturità* exams in their chosen fields may move on to university. Most university students will have been to a *liceo* but it is also possible to go to university from a vocational school.

International schools

Children from foreign countries integrate well into Italian schools if they are very young – at nursery or primary school age. Older children will naturally be apprehensive about having to cope with a new language, new country, new school and new friends. As a parent you must decide if your child can cope with such a huge change. You may decide that it would be better to stick with a familiar school system and curriculum by enrolling him or her in one of the international schools. Your child will still learn Italian and hopefully become bilingual but he or she will be instructed in their own language, which will be much less confusing. In making this decision, parents will have to be mindful about the proximity of such schools to where they live and for how long they intend to live in Italy. If your company has sent you to Italy for only a couple of years, it is obviously not advisable to switch from one school system to another.

International schools operate in the main Italian cities such as Rome, Florence and Milan and they follow the American, British or International Baccalaureate curriculum. All follow educational programmes that will prepare students for university. Advice and a list of schools can be obtained from the European Council of International Schools on www.ecis.org or write to the organization at 21B Lavant Street, Petersfield, Hampshire GU32 3EL, England.

University

The oldest university in Italy is in Bologna. It was established in the 11th century and there is a joke that some of the original students are still studying there because they don't want to rush into finishing their degree courses. Italian students take a long time to finish university – some may not graduate until they are in their late twenties – and their indulgent parents are expected to support them financially during this time. The reason for this is that degree courses are long to start with – four to six years – but students can elongate their period of study if they want, and if they fail any exam they can re-take it as many times as necessary. Italian parents do not expect their children to start a career as early as young people do in other countries. When my 23-year-old stepson was visiting recently, my Italian friends were amazed that he had already graduated from university and had been working for a year. 'Poor boy! You should have let him breathe! He needs to relax after all that study!' was the general opinion.

Any student with a diploma from *scuola superiore* can apply to study the subject of their choice, as long as there are places available. Students are required to pass entrance exams for popular subjects such as architecture, medicine and dentistry so that the best candidates can be given places. Assessment of work during the degree course is again both oral and written. In order to graduate, students must write a thesis and present it to a board of 11 professors.

There are many opportunities for foreign students to study at Italian universities. Every year the Italian Ministry of Foreign Affairs offers British and American citizens, with good knowledge of the Italian language, scholarships to study at prestigious universities such as Siena or Perugia. The Italian Cultural Institute in London, which also offers occasional study scholarships, has details on its Web site at www.italcultur.org.uk, or contact the Italian embassy in your own country. British and American universities with Italian language departments also have links with their counterparts in Italy and can offer periods of study as part of a degree course. The Erasmus scholarship programme offers grants to study in Italy, giving financial help to cover the cost of flights and accommodation.

The Open University in Italy

You can study at the OU while in Italy. There are more than 150 courses to choose from – arts, social sciences, technology, business management, mathematics, education, science, computing, etc. If you are semi-retired in Italy or want to increase your career opportunities while living here, this may be your chance to do so. All courses are in English and you study in your own time at home, supported by multi-media course material and tutoring. Apply for more information to Jane Pollard, The Open University, CP 1141, Milan, Tel: 0281 38048 or e-mail J.Pollard@open.ac.uk. For the Open University Business School contact Tim O'Donnel, Tel: 04 99338849 or e-mail T.A.Odonnell@open.ac.uk.

Health

The standard of medical care in Italy is generally good with dedicated and highly trained health professionals in the *Servizio Sanitario Nazionale* (SSN). It is the state hospitals that let the system down – standards will vary region by region with the poorest resources in the south – but hospital staff are over-worked and under pressure, there is a lack of privacy in wards and the food can be abominable. Families of the sick may be expected to help out with some general looking-after of their loved ones – it all sounds a lot like the British National Health Service. The quality of medical treatment, however, is good. There are more doctors in Italy than in the UK and you generally have complete freedom of choice over the doctor you want and to go directly to a specialist, without a GP referral, if you know what is wrong with you. There are waiting lists for some types of treatment but you will be treated immediately if you have cancer or a similar serious health problem. Indeed, Italy has some of the best cancer hospitals in the world.

Medical insurance

Many Italians and most foreigners, however, also have medical insurance over and above state cover so that they can see specialists of their choosing ahead of the waiting list. This also means that they can have in-patient treatment in clinics that supply comforts such as private rooms and en-suite bathrooms. Health insurance companies in your own country can provide this kind of medical cover through a Europe-wide policy. The *Istituto Nazionale delle Assicurazioni,* whose number you will find in the Italian Yellow Pages, also provides private cover. If you do have a private health care plan, it is standard procedure to pay up front for all consultations, x-rays and prescriptions and then reclaim the money.

Medical treatment for foreigners

There is a reciprocal agreement among member states of the European Community that entitles all EU citizens on a temporary stay in Italy to treatment if they or their dependants are suddenly taken ill or have an accident. You will receive the same treatment as an Italian national. This is suitable for people who have holiday homes and will only be in Italy a few weeks a year, but you may want to top it up with private insurance, particularly if you have specific health problems. To qualify for this you must apply for an E111 form before arrival in Italy. Go to any main post office or travel agent and ask for a leaflet called 'Health Advice for Travellers'. Fill in the form and have it stamped and signed by the post office or you will not be able to use it. Keep the original with your passport and have at least one extra photocopy, as you will be required to hand over the photocopy to a hospital or clinic. There is no time limit to an E111 form but make sure you keep it up to date – for example, if you change address or there are additions to your family. Young people over the age of 19 must have their own E111 form.

Depending on the treatment necessary, go to the *Pronto Soccorso* (casualty unit) of the nearest hospital or ask for advice from the local health unit (*Unita Sanitaria Locale)* The USL will examine your E111, provide you with a certificate and give you a list of doctors who subscribe to the scheme. You may have to pay a small fee for the consultation, which is not refundable. For prescribed medicines, you will also have to pay a non-refundable charge. If the doctor thinks you need hospital treatment he or she will give you a *proposto di ricovero* that will entitle you to treatment at specified hospitals. Again, depending on which part of Italy you are in, you may have to pay a fee. Keep all receipts or you will not be able to claim a refund. The Department of Health in the UK advises that if you are unable to contact a USL first, you should show the hospital authorities your E111 and ask them to contact the local office to determine your rights to treatment.

Refund of costs incurred

To claim a refund of costs you can apply to the authorities in Italy or wait until you are back in the UK. Send all original documents with a covering letter to: Department for Work and Pensions Benefits Agency, Overseas Division Medical Benefits, Tyneview Park, Whitley Road, Newcastle upon Tyne, NE98 1BA, or telephone 0191 218 7547; the office is open to enquiries from 8am until 4pm. Note that emergency renal dialysis is covered under this scheme. If you receive a UK state pension and live in Italy, you are entitled to treatment without making any contribution. You will need to ask the British authorities for a form 121 to establish your entitlement.

Non-EU citizens must make arrangements for private medical insurance cover and ask advice from their embassy or consulate.

Living in Italy

You are not entitled to use the E111 form if you are living permanently in Italy. You must apply to the USL, also sometimes called A*zienda Sanitaria Locale (ASL)*, for your green health card that enrols you in the Italian health service. Take your passport and your residency papers to the local health authority. You can choose which doctor to register with – ask friends, your employer or the local consulate for advice. Many doctors in the Italian health service speak English because they have worked in the UK or the USA, so you may want to track down someone with whom you can communicate fully. You will be encouraged to make a well-patient visit and thereafter will be able to visit your doctor at his *ambulatorio* (surgery) on a first-come, first-served basis during surgery hours. He will prescribe medicines and refer you to specialists, if necessary. If you are from an EU country your green medical card will be valid for five years.

Dentists

If you are an EU citizen you are entitled to cost-reduced dental treatment, but most people opt to pay for treatment privately.

Opticians

If you need a sight test you can simply make an appointment with an *ottico* (optician) of your choice. Prices of spectacles and contact lenses are on a par with the rest of Europe. If you are registered with the *Servizio Nazionale Sanitaria* and develop serious eye problems, you can ask your doctor to refer you to an eye specialist.

Pharmacies

Pharmacies are usually small family-run businesses in Italy. You will see them in any small town or village, distinguished by a large green neon cross in front of the shop. There are some 24-hour pharmacies in the main cities, but most pharmacies keep normal working hours, closing for lunch. Consult local newspapers, where pharmacy opening times are published. You will be able to ask the pharmacists for advice on minor ailments such as insect bites, colds or flu. You can also buy a *test di gravidanza* (pregnancy testing kit) over the counter as well as some medicines that would normally require a prescription in your home country.

Vaccinations

No vaccinations are required to enter Italy. Children must be immunized against tetanus, polio, diphtheria and hepatitis B. You will need copies of these vaccination certificates when enrolling your child at an Italian school.

Pregnancy and childbirth

Italy has a high standard of prenatal care. Ultrasound examinations, gynaecological services and a three-day hospital stay are covered by the *Servizio Nazionale Sanitaria*, if you are registered. Giving birth in a private clinic will cost approximately 3,000 euros but it may be wiser to use a public hospital since clinics do not have comprehensive emergency care. Fathers or other members of the family are encouraged to be present at the birth. It is possible, but not usual, to arrange a home birth and you may be asked to pay if you want this service. Postnatal care for the child in the first four weeks, if needed, is provided by the obstetric team and afterwards by the family doctor or nurse. Non-Italians should make sure they have pregnancy reference books in their own language so that they can follow what the doctor is telling them. A new baby must be registered at the *comune* within 10 days of birth and babies are given regular medical checkups until the age of 24 months. Parents will be sent written reminders about immunisation.

Letting and selling your Italian home

Letting

Letting your property is a way of recovering some of the cost of buying and restoring your house, but to be successful you need to ensure that your property is geared to the relatively sophisticated needs of Italian renters. Do not assume that you can patch up an old barn on your property, stick in a couple of bedrooms and a bathroom with an electric shower, and watch the rental income roll in. People are extremely fussy about where they spend their precious Italian fortnight and they will not accept sub-standard accommodation under the guise of it being a 'rustic' house. This point was perfectly illustrated in the television programme 'A Year in Tuscany' when the young couple who were the stars of the series found out that the rented accommodation they had built and were so proud of was not up to standard. The first guests walked out and booked accommodation elsewhere.

The main clientele in the Italian market are middle-class British families, well-heeled Americans, Germans and Scandinavians, and they have high expectations. The more facilities you offer, therefore, the more you will be able to charge and the greater number of clients you will attract. Properties that have facilities such as ISDN lines, Sky TV, a cook and maid service, heated pool, etc, can command higher prices in what is a competitive and crowded market.

You can let your home yourself or go through an agency. Whichever route you choose, it is very important that in the Web site/brochure there is a detailed description of the property and as many photographs as possible. This leads back to the point about people's expectations – when they are not met, the situation can turn quite ugly. For example, a couple rented the house of friends of mine and complained at the end of their stay, asking for their money back. They said the rental agency had over-egged the description of the house and griped that the property was not as grand as they had imagined it would be. Instead of antiques, they found simple, painted Italian country furniture that my friends had restored. It is a beautiful house but it was not what these people were expecting and so, they were not happy. It is best to have as full and as accurate a description as possible so that prospective renters know exactly what they are coming to.

Information pack

You should prepare an information pack on the house and the area – in particular, give concise instructions on how to reach the house and include maps and diagrams. Prepare a list of nearby restaurants, supermarkets, banks, pharmacies, worthwhile sightseeing trips and other local tourist attractions such as water theme parks for children. Also prepare a list of emergency numbers such as local hospitals, dentists and visiting doctors.

Creating a Web site – advertising

If you are planning to try to rent your property yourself it will be worthwhile to create a Web site so that potential clients can take a virtual tour to see if this is where they want to spend their holidays. The cost is not too high these days – about £500 – and it will be a worthwhile investment. You can also advertise your property in the Sunday supplements – submit the advert in the early new year when people are dreaming of sunshine and lazy summer days. If you work for a large company, a hospital or local authority, or have friends who do, put up a notice in the canteen or rest room. Use other informal advertising means such as a postcard in your local church or sports club. Ask friends to pass the word around that you have a gorgeous property in Italy for private rental.

Letting contract

Look at the contracts offered by professional letting agencies and use them as a guide for your own. If you want to specify conditions such as no smoking or no pets, make that clear in the contract. You should ask for 50 per cent of the cost as an advance deposit and ensure that the remaining 50 per cent is paid a maximum two weeks before arrival. Secure a deposit against damages that may be incurred and do not repay it until you are completely happy that all the costs have been cleared. For example, clients may say they will use their own mobile phones, but you will have to check your telephone bill and show them the itemized calls and relevant dates if it turns out they have been using the main line as well.

If you are renting out your own home during periods when you are not in Italy, keep a cupboard or walk-in room where you are can lock away your best china, silk cushions, valuable books and other personal items. Expect a certain amount of wear and tear – even the best clients will break glasses or ruin cushions by sitting on them in wet swimsuits, so put personal items beyond harm's reach. The saving grace is that people who come to Italy are generally well behaved – the lager louts go elsewhere.

Appointing a rental agent

There are dozens of English-speaking management agents who actively search for new rental properties in Italy each season. They all have Web sites or brochures. The main thing is to find agents who like the style of your house, who have the sort of clientele to whom it will appeal, and who will pitch it at the right price. The agents will advise you of what the weekly rental should be. You will need to keep an eye on whichever company you choose and ensure that its staff are keeping the property as fully let as possible – ask for regular reports, especially as high season approaches. A management company will probably charge about 20 per cent of the rental income plus VAT, so you have the right to be demanding.

Costs

You will not make your fortune by renting out your Italian property. A yearly return of about 7 per cent is all that you should expect, but renting will cover costs and upkeep of the property. You must factor in the price of cleaning and maintenance (maid, gardener and pool person), household insurance, advertising, telephone and stationery costs as well as wear and tear and other incidental damage.

Local help

It is important to have someone locally who can sort out problems if you are not in Italy. A maid or gardener should have a list of workmen when things go wrong, as they do all the time – no hot water, the washing machine doesn't spin, the *pozzo* has gone dry, etc. Someone has to be able to deal with these events and call you if things are serious. It is recommended that someone like a maid should go in every day just to see what is going on, for example, that clients have not brought more guests than they said they would bring, that they are treating the house with respect, and that children are not kicking footballs around the house or getting up to other mischief. This person should also be on hand to answer any queries the guests may have. When renters arrive there should be some basic supplies – bread, water, milk, orange juice and wine in the fridge – to welcome them.

Approach the letting of your property as a business. Remember that as owners you will have to be on call at all times – either in person or at the end of a telephone. All guests should be declared at the *comune;* this was traditionally an anti-terrorist measure, but many people do not bother doing this any more. If you have large and regular numbers of guests, it is best to keep on the right side of the law and your letting agency may do this for you. Income from your letting your property should be declared, whether you are living in Italy or your home country. An accountant will advise you.

Lettings, unfurnished

Letting your unfurnished house in Italy to another person is not to be taken lightly. In Chapter 3 I explained that the law provides a lot of protection for tenants in unfurnished properties. If you decide to let out your unfurnished property, your tenant has a right to stay there for at least four years. Getting back your property, unless there are very good reasons such as substantial rent arrears, is all but impossible.

If you are happy with these terms you are entitled to hold a deposit (*cauzione*) against any damages that may occur. This is usually two months' rental and it must be held in an interest-bearing bank account and returned, less any sums owed by the tenant, at the end of the rental agreement period.

As a landlord you are responsible for major repairs to the building such as roofing, windows, chimney, etc, and your tenants are responsible for repairs inside the property such as plumbing, painting and decorating, etc. The responsibilities on both sides can be made clear in the rental contract.

Lettings, furnished

It might be best, if you do want to let your property for a long period, to rent it on a furnished basis. This means fully furnished, with everything a person would need to live comfortably, save for personal linen, cutlery and china. Furnished property is subject to less stringent conditions and you will be able to negotiate a rental period of anything from a week to a few years. This is much better for you as the landlord because it leaves you with more control over the property and your tenant.

Selling your property

If you decide to sell your Italian house, you will probably sell it through an estate agent or a *mediatore*. An estate agent will charge 3 per cent commission. He may ask you to sign an exclusivity contract – don't. This would mean that if the house is sold through someone else, he could still claim his commission. You can instruct several estate agents and see who comes in with the best offer first. It is common for people to instruct different estate agents, and to give them different prices, as a way of testing the market. But it is not advisable – ask two or three agents to come and look at the house and give their valuation. Don't be carried away by someone who promises you the earth – go for the agent who has a good track record and who has priced your house according to your own ideas of its value. A *mediatore* is not really an estate agent; he will have other businesses on the go. He acts as a go-between between seller and agent and possible purchaser, taking his commission where he can. You probably wouldn't use a *mediatore* unless he was a friend or someone who had been properly recommended.

Most people who sell their property sell it on to other expatriates, largely because most Italians cannot afford these kinds of properties. In addition, the seller has probably never declared to the tax authorities in his home country that he has a holiday home and, because he is selling to another foreigner, the sale takes place outside of Italy and 'under-the-table'. Therefore, the tax implications can be fudged.

There is no longer any capital gains tax on property in Italy, but you should consult an accountant or *commercialista* to look at your individual situation.

Working and setting up a business in Italy

Working in Italy

The Italian government is allowed to reserve certain posts for their nationals if the jobs require the exercise of powers conferred by law and the safeguarding of the country's interests, for example the judiciary, the diplomatic service, the police and the armed forces. Apart from that, most other public sector jobs in health and education, and in industry and all commercial services are entirely open to citizens of the EU member countries; they are entitled to live and work anywhere within the Union. Other nationalities should consult their embassies in their home country or in Italy to find out their eligibility to work and if they will have to apply for work permits.

The crucial factor in securing employment in Italy is, of course, mastery of the language. In theory an EU citizen should be treated in exactly the same way as an Italian national when seeking employment, but in practice this does not happen. Not being proficient in the Italian language will count against you. If a job is between you and an Italian, it is not unreasonable for the employer to choose the person he or she and their customers will be able to communicate with. There are some people who can get away with living in Italy without speaking much Italian. They work for multinational companies in cities like Milan and Rome and speak English during their working day, but these kinds of jobs are in the minority. I repeat, to find employment you will have to get cracking on those language lessons. It will be important at the very least to demonstrate to an Italian employer that you have a reasonable knowledge of Italian and are willing to improve it.

Before you go to Italy

You can start to job hunt before you arrive in Italy. Research job opportunities within your own particular profession, look at trade magazines and see if there are any companies of a similar nature already established in Italy. Remember that Italy's main industries are tourism, textiles, ceramics, car manufacturing, iron and steel production, engineering and agriculture, so if you have skills in those areas you have a head start.

If you are a British citizen you can write for advice on Italian job opportunities to The Employment Service, Overseas Placing Unit, Level 4, Skills House, 3–7 Holy Green, Off The Moor, Sheffield S1 4AQ, Tel: 0114 259 6051, Web site: www.employmentservice.gov.uk. The Italian government's job-searching Web site is: www.welfare.gov.it (click on the relevant logo on the left hand side of the home page, *incontro/domanda/offerta di lavoro*).

If you are an EU citizen you can contact European Employment Services (EURES), a network whose purpose is to facilitate the mobility of workers within the European Economic Area. EURES has 500 Euroadvisors whose role is to provide information about rights and working conditions, advice and placement assistance for jobseekers and for employers interested in the international job market. The EURES Web site will give you information about job conditions in Italy as well as a useful fact-sheet entitled 'Looking for Work'. You can call a freephone number from the UK, 0800 581591, or visit the Web site: www.europa.eu.int/jobs/eures.

When you arrive in Italy

As a first step you could try finding work among the expatriate community in Italy. Other foreigners will obviously be sympathetic to any language problems that a new arrival will have, having experienced it themselves, and may be willing to take you on. Ask around on the expatriate grapevine or put a personal ad in a magazine, such as *Wanted in Rome* or the online magazine *The Informer,* offering your services. In cities like Rome, Florence and Milan, companies such as estate agencies, legal practices and international charities seek secretaries with English as their mother tongue and an understanding of Italian. You can also have a go at sending your CV to some of the big, multinational companies; here's an example with the Italian language version of the main headings:

Nome (first name)   *Cognome* (last name)

Luogo e data di nascita (place and date of birth)

Domicilio attuale (current address)

Numero telefonico (telephone number)

E-mail

Stato civile (married, single, etc)

Curriculum scolastico (educational history)

Corsi post-universitari (qualifications after university)

Esperienze di lavoro precedenti (work experience)

Lingue parlate (languages spoken)

Hobbies

Referenze (names of people who will act as character referees)

If you do get an interview, speak in Italian as much as possible, even if it is only a few words and phrases that you have learnt by heart. Prepare a few sentences about the skills that you have, why you have come to live in Italy and what you think you can contribute. Do not dress casually – Italians are quite formal and will not take you seriously if you turn up for a job interview in jeans or shorts. They will expect you to be well groomed and to wear the proper attire even if it is 40 degrees outside. Address your interviewer by his or her title, do not use their first name, and try not to show that you are nervous or unsure of yourself. Project confidence with a firm handshake, and a direct gaze, and show that you are serious about making a success of your new life in Italy.

Another resource for job hunters is Italy's newspapers, which publish job advertisements. The Friday edition of *Corriere della Sera* has a situations vacant supplement; you could also examine the jobs advertised in the *International Herald Tribune* and the *Wall Street Journal Europe*. Local newspapers print job advertisements on particular days of the week.

Young people may want to try working in a hotel, restaurant or bar. Many hotels, especially the big branded ones, require people who speak English for reception work and are quite used to staff seeking employment to improve their language skills. If you are looking for work outside a big city, you should approach some of the bigger *agriturismos* that cater for tourists and may require chambermaids or restaurant and reception staff. Young people can also contact *informagiovani* centres about employment and help in finding training courses and enrolment in colleges or universities – visit www.informagiovani.it.

Being paid in cash

A warning word about the 'black economy'. Many small businesses in Italy operate partly in cash since it saves them paying IVA and will reduce the proprietor's income tax liability. If you are paid in cash you have, as an under-the-counter employee, no protection if you fall ill, have an accident or experience any other kind of mishap. Your boss can sack you, your salary can be reduced, your terms of work changed and your holiday entitlement slashed and there will not be very much that you can do about it. It would be naive to say not to take on a job that pays in cash – it is a common way of starting out in Italy – but keep this in mind. Do not do any dangerous casual jobs, such as working on a building site, as you will not be insured.

Jobcentres and private employment agencies

Jobseekers can visit the jobcentres run by the Italian government's employment agencies *(ufficio di collocamento manodopera);* look in the telephone directory or ask at the local *commune* for the nearest one to where you live. If you are an EU citizen you should receive the same kind of advice and assistance in finding employment as that available for Italians. There are private employment agencies dealing mostly in secretarial vacancies in Italy and you will also find their contact details in the telephone directory under *Lavoro Internale e Temporaneo*. To sign up with an agency you will need a *permesso di soggiorno, codice fiscale* and *libretto di lavoro*. There are also executive recruitment agencies that search specifically for management personnel; see under *ricerca personale*.

Language teaching

Many foreigners resort to teaching English as a way to earn money in Italy. They take a TEFL (Teaching English as a Foreign Language) course in their own country or when they arrive in Italy, and they seek work in one of the hundreds of language schools dotted about the country, or they find their own pupils for private classes. This is certainly a good way of supporting yourself in the beginning, but the rates of pay for language teaching are abysmal, the work uncertain and seasonal and the competition for pupils is considerable. This is not suitable year-round employment. By all means, start off in this way but regard it as a short-term solution. You cannot rely on earning enough through language teaching to support a decent lifestyle in Italy.

Equivalence of qualifications

If you are a potter, a jewellery maker or some other kind of artisan, you do not need to equalize any technical qualifications from your home country in order to work in Italy. You will either be setting up business on your own or you will simply have to demonstrate the range of your skills to gain a position with an employer.

If you are in a regulated profession such as teaching, nursing or the law you must apply for recognition of your qualifications in order to gain work. For example, there are English-qualified dentists and doctors working in the big Italian cities and they must by law be re-accredited by the Italian authorities. Once this is done they are given an authorization number and can start practising. The best way to find out about equivalence of qualifications is to ask your professional trade body for advice – this can and should be done from the UK several months ahead of your arrival. Alternatively, you can ask a relocation service, whose number you will find in the English *Yellow Pages*, to help you wade through the Italian bureaucracy. The EURES staff will also be able to advise you on this point.

In some occupations such as hairdresser or construction worker, you may only need to prove length of employment to confirm your level of proficiency, or you may have to sit practical exams in order to re-qualify for work in Italy. If you are a plumber or electrician, you cannot legally start working in Italy without going through the formalities. These are regulated professions and you will have to prove your expertise by sitting exams and being assessed. Again, trade bodies are the best places to start with this kind of inquiry.

You can also contact the Department of Trade and Industry, 1 Victoria Street, London SW1H, Tel: 020 7215 5000, Web site www.dti.gov.uk, about recognition of qualifications. The British Council and British Chamber of Commerce in Italy will also have useful information (see Useful Addresses).

Unemployment benefit

If you have been out of work in the UK and want to move to Italy you can continue to receive your Jobseeker's Allowance for up to 13 weeks. You must have been registered as a jobseeker for at least four weeks before you left the UK and have been available for work up until your departure. You must tell your Jobcentre before leaving and complete the appropriate E303 form. You must register at an Italian jobcentre within seven days of your arrival. If you cannot find work during the 13-week period, you will have to return to the UK if you wish to continue to receive your benefits. You are entitled to the three-month payment only once between two periods of employment.

Working conditions in Italy

The unemployment rate in Italy, at the time of writing, is running at 9 per cent. Jobless rates are twice as high in parts of the less developed *Mezzogiorno* in the south of Italy. Depending on the company, employees are eligible for up to 28 days holiday plus 11 bank holidays and Easter Monday off. It is difficult to quantify the minimum wage in Italy since salaries are collectively bargained between employers and unions and there are 140 categories of employment, and therefore 140 minimum wages. To make things even more complicated, there is the difference between a minimum wage in the north of Italy and a minimum wage in the south. On average, however, a minimum wage is 500 euros a month, not a lot to survive on! Firms give a month's salary as a bonus at Christmas – it is called the 13th month. Tax and social security is deducted at source. Many Italians do not earn enough and therefore they have second occupations or additional sources of income, such as working part-time in the family business, selling wine or olive oil, or renting out property.

Setting up a business in Italy

Every country has complex rules and regulations about the establishment of a business and Italy is no exception. The country's infamous bureaucracy seems at its worst in this field and to complicate matters even further, new corporate reform has been introduced in January 2004 – the first big changes in Italy in about 60 years. Therefore, if you are thinking about setting up a small business, you would be best advised to seek specialist advice. There are dual qualified law practices that specialize in the field of commercial and corporate law. They can give advice to non-Italians setting up commercial ventures, large and small, and money spent on their fees will probably be a wise investment. At the very least you will need to find a notary with whom you can communicate because he will be the person who will be doing all the paperwork.

Most expatriates who move to Italy want to set up businesses related to the tourist trade. Making and selling pottery, becoming a tour guide, running art classes, opening a bed and breakfast or *agriturismo,* or functioning as an estate agent are just a few examples of the kind of work you can do. If you can, try to work as an employee in the type of business that you want to open. Even it is only for a few weeks or a few months – and even if you are not being paid very well or not at all – it will give you invaluable experience. You may decide to run a mile from opening that bar or that bed and breakfast. This kind of work experience will tell you if your expectations for your business in Italy are realistic or if they are too high – it could end up saving you considerable money and heartache. Be aware that many small businesses fail because their owners have not properly researched the market in Italy, under-estimated start-up costs, or been too optimistic about how much profit they can make. For a very good insight into the pros and cons of running B and Bs and *agriturismos* you should look at the online magazine *The Informer*, which has covered this subject in depth.

What type of company should I set up?

The Italian Civil Code allows for many different business structures, which are divided into two categories – an individual enterprise for sole traders, and a collective enterprise where a group of people join together in business. Each has its own particular characteristics.

Individual enterprise

This is for the sole trader *(imprenditore)*, where one person is carrying out the business activity. This person takes all the decisions relating to the company – how, where, what and how much to produce, sales prices, contacting suppliers, etc. He or she can collaborate with other independent workers or employees, but they do not have any decisional power. The sole trader has unlimited liability towards debts derived from the performance of this business, which will be covered from his or her own assets. Should the sole trader become insolvent therefore, he or she would be declared bankrupt. This kind of enterprise is very straightforward to set up – it needs only to be registered in the relevant section of the Business Register *(Registro delle Imprese)* kept by the local Chamber of Commerce. For people who plan to work from home, this may be the simplest and easiest route. But seek professional advice so that you can be sure that this is the best option for your individual situation.

Collective enterprise

This is when two or more people want to set up in business and where there may be shareholder involvement and profit-sharing. The two main options are to run the business as a partnership or as a company.

If you opt to run your business as a *partnership,* no minimum capital is required and each member's interest is called a 'quota' and depends on the amount of capital contributed or the services provided. Creditors can enforce their claim against individual members only after the execution on the assets of the partnership. The different types of partnership are:

■ Unlimited Partnership – *Società in Nome Collettivo (Snc)* is where all members are jointly liable for the partnership's debts and obligations without limit. At least one of the partners must include his or her name in the title of the company.

■ Limited Partnership – *Società in Accomandita Semplice (Sas)* is where non-managing members can limit the amount of their liability if they are not involved in the day-to-day decisions of the partnership.

■ Simple Partnership – *Società Semplice* is where two or more partners work together without strictly performing a commercial trading activity. For example, a group of farmers may work together in a

Società Semplice. Profits and losses of the partnership are shared, depending on the size of each partner's contribution.

Under the Italian Civil Code all *companies* must be enrolled on the Business Register and each type of company must provide a minimum capital required by Italian law. Members' financial obligations are limited to the extent of their subscribed shares. The different types of companies are:

I Limited Liability Company – *Società a Responsabilita Limitata (Srl)* is like a private company in the UK and is generally used by small or medium-sized businesses in Italy. It has a minimum authorized capital of 10,000 euros and 25 per cent of this amount (2,500 euros) must be paid up and deposited with a bank prior to incorporation. Directors need not be Italian citizens or full-time residents in Italy and their voting rights depend on their respective financial input to the capital or their contribution to the company in terms of service. It is possible for small entrepreneurs to open a single-member *Srl* – to do so, the minimum capital of 10,000 euros must be entirely paid up and it must be made clear in publicity required by law that the business is a single-member limited company.

I Company Limited by Shares – *Società per Azioni (SpA)* is normally for large-scale business enterprises. The minimum subscribed capital is 100,000 euros of which at least 30,000 euros must be paid up and deposited with a bank prior to incorporation. Shareholders may be individuals or corporations, and a board of statutory auditors chosen from the *Registro dei Revisori Contabili* must supervise the management of the company to ensure compliance with the law and to verify the company accounts.

I Unlimited Company – *Società in Accomandita per Azioni (SApA)*, the minimum subscribed capital is 100,000 euros, which is divided into shares. At least one of the managing members must have his or her name in the title of the company. Managing members are liable to the full extent of their assets; non-managing members have limited liability.

I Cooperative – *Società Cooperativa* is for groups of traders who want to join together to provide goods and services inexpensively. Cooperatives must be registered at the local Chamber of Commerce and can be formed with limited or unlimited liability.

Other ways of doing business

It is possible to trade goods through an Italian agent who will charge commission, to open a branch office in Italy of your existing company, or to set up a representative office in Italy. Obviously, these methods of doing business have tax implications and you would need professional advice on whether or not this is feasible for you.

Business taxes

Businesses in Italy are subject to direct and indirect taxation systems. The main taxes to be aware of are:

▌ Corporate income tax – *Imposta sul Reddito delle Società (IRES)* is a proportional tax with a fixed rate, which is being lowered from 36 to 33 per cent with the new financial reforms. The tax authorities request advance payments and the deadlines are on the twentieth day of the sixth month following the closing of the financial year (full settlement of tax due from the previous year and a first instalment) and the end of the eleventh month of the current tax period (payment of a second or single instalment).

▌ Regional Tax on Productive Activities – *Imposta sul Reddito delle Attivita Produttive (IRAP)* – most traders and businesses have to pay this tax, which is 4.25 per cent of net production. The tax rate is cut to 3.10 per cent in the case of farmers. The exceptions are people earning income generated by occasional independent work or earned from collaborations performed on a coordinated and continuous basis.

▌ Value Added Tax – *Imposta sul Valore Aggiunto (IVA)* is a tax levied on the added value of goods in each individual phase of production and distribution. It is charged to the consumer, who pays the entire tax. IVA is generally levied on imports, transfers of goods and supplies of services carried out during the performance of business, artistic or professional activities. IVA rates vary from 4 to 20 per cent depending on the goods or services under consideration; 20 per cent is the most common rate.

▌ Registration Tax – *Imposta di Registro* is applicable to all documents and contracts written in Italy and is assessed as a percentage or a fixed fee. It is also applicable to the purchase of property, with rates ranging from 3 to 15 per cent, or sales of a business, with a rate of 3 per cent.

❚ Council Tax on Property – *Imposta Communale sugli Immobili (ICI)* is levied on homeowners and also on owners of business properties, with rates ranging from 0.4 to 0.7 per cent of the property's value.

Social charges

Employers are required by law to register their employees with the National Institute for Social Security (INPS) or the equivalent National Institutes for particular kinds of employment. Social security and welfare contributions cover healthcare, state pensions, disability, maternity leave and family allowances. Self-employed workers such as artisans, shopkeepers and self-employed farm workers pay their own contributions.

Grants and assistance

Aid packages and financial incentives for setting up new businesses in Italy are available from local, regional and central government as well as from the EU. Incentives mainly consist of tax breaks, labour cost inducements, loans at subsidized rates and cash grants. You may be able to get financial assistance, for example, if you are a female entrepreneur or a young entrepreneur. People who want to open businesses of any size in specific geographical areas, such as the south of Italy where unemployment is high, can receive a lot of help in establishing a new venture. The key, of course, is finding out how to access these kinds of grants. As a first step, you should contact the list of organizations below.

Organizations that can help

The British Chamber of Commerce in Italy (BCCI) is a private, non-profit-making organization that assists people who want to set up business in Italy. The headquarters are in Milan and there are branches in Emilia-Romagna, Tuscany, Lazio, Liguria, Sardinia, Piedmont, Veneto, Friuli-Venezia-Guilia, Puglia and Campania. An annual individual membership costs 248 euros. The BCCI can advise you – in English – on all aspects of establishing a new commercial venture in Italy. It also has a network of useful people you can call upon – lawyers, accountants, other businessmen and women (see Useful Addresses).

The British Consulate-General in Milan is responsible for all commercial and inward investment business. It provides an extensive range of services to help UK companies develop their business in Italy (see Useful Addresses).

The Italian Trade Commission and the Italian Chamber of Commerce, both in London, offer their services free to any company that wants to locate its business in Italy. They will also advise lone traders (see Useful Addresses).

Bank finance

If you are seeking a loan from a bank to finance your business, you will need to present a well-thought-out business plan, assessing the demand for your product or service, the predicted revenue and costs. You will also have to disclose what assets are going into the business and give details of your personal financial situation. As always, you are more likely to impress a bank manager if you show a good command of Italian and a good local knowledge of your area. In Italy there are trade associations that can offer loans at more attractive rates and these organizations would require the same financial information.

Taxation

It has been said that Italians regard laws as mere suggestions, and this describes very well the Italian attitude to paying taxes. Tax evasion is practically a national sport in Italy and a substantial part of the nation's economy is run on the black market. However, everybody has to pay at least the basic taxes. Major fiscal reform is currently under way in Italy, the tax situation is in a state of flux, and the following information should be taken only as a general guide.

Tax forms

In Italy you have to 'declare' yourself – that is, you have to fill in your own tax declaration, deduct allowances and credits and then submit the sum that you think you owe. The *intendenza di finanza* will not remind you to do this, so it is every individual's responsibility. Tax forms are available from accountants, office stationery shops and newsagents. Some financial publications offer them free; normally you will have to pay a small charge for them.

Liability for income tax

Liability for Italian income tax depends on whether you are resident in Italy or not. You are deemed liable for income tax if any of the following applies:

- your permanent or principal residence is in Italy;
- you spend more than 183 days in Italy during any calendar year;
- your principal employment is in Italy;
- your centre of vital economic interest, eg investments or business, is in Italy.

Generally speaking, all income earned in Italy, even by non-residents, is taxable in Italy. So if a foreign arts company comes to do a concert here, the fee ought to be paid net of withholding tax.

You do not have to make a personal income tax declaration if you are in the following categories:

■ you have no income;
■ you are on PAYE and have no other income;
■ your income is a war, old age or invalidity pension that is exempt from tax;
■ you have already paid tax at source on dividends, bank interest, mortgage interest, etc.

Income tax for house-owners

As a house-owner, there are three different scenarios that you must look at. Each one is described below.

Scenario 1

If you are buying a house in Italy but your main residence and place of work are outside the country, and you are not going to derive an income from renting out the house, then the tax you need to be aware of is property tax (ICI); see below. Some comunes raise additional taxation in relation to the services that they supply to people in their area. The amount for this will be based on how big your house is. It may include rubbish collection, the cleaning of the streets and keeping beaches in order. The sums involved are not generally high.

Scenario 2

You have bought a house in Italy, your main residence and place of work are outside Italy, but you rent out your house as extra income. If you let your house you have to declare the income received. You are able to offset certain expenses against that income – maintenance, management, expenses, local taxes, etc, and the remainder – the profit – is taxed at between 19 and 46 per cent, depending on the amounts involved. The average appears to be around 30 per cent. Because of a treaty between Italy and the UK, double taxation relief exists, so although you will have to declare the income to the British tax authorities, you should not be taxed upon it twice. You will also have to pay *ICI* and any other local taxes for rubbish collection, cleaning, etc.

Scenario 3

You are living and working in Italy. The Italian tax year is the same as the calendar year and if you are employed in Italy your tax is paid via a PAYE system where employees' tax is deducted at the workplace by the employers. Everyone is taxed individually and if you are married, you are still taxed as individuals, not as a couple. For the tax authorities, income is based on the sum of all possible sources of income – land, capital, dependent and independent occupations, enterprises and other sources owned by subjects. A new form of allowances and tax deductions is being introduced which is meant to simplify the system and lower the overall amount of tax due. It remains to be seen whether this will work in practice. Deductions from taxable income will be applied to low and medium-level incomes, diminishing as incomes increase. Also taken into account will be the type of family in terms of the number of children, elderly and disabled dependants, housing conditions, other factors such as health and education, training schemes, social security and welfare, research and cultural activities, non-profit activities, all activities performed in the social and voluntary work fields, religious creeds and expenses incurred in pursuit of business.

Rates of tax

Up until recently the rates of tax depending upon income were 18, 24, 32, 39 or 45 per cent. At the time of writing a new tax (IRE) is replacing the five bands with only two. These are 23 per cent for incomes up to 100,000 euros and 33 per cent for incomes over 100,000 euros. There will also be a no-tax area based on a minimum personal income exempt from taxation. There are stiff financial penalties for not paying your personal income tax on time. You will also have to pay yearly *ICI* and other local taxes.

Employing the services of a *commercialista*

For someone who is new to Italy, dealing with all the various taxes is quite a task and so most foreigners, and many Italians, employ the services of a *commercialista*, who is an accountant. He or she is an expert in tax affairs and will tell you if you need to fill in a declaration and will fill it in on your behalf if you do. He or she will advise you on all the allowances and credits that you can offset against tax. This is particularly useful if you are self-employed, as your tax situation will obviously be more complicated. Ask around for a recommended *commercialista* – even the smallest Italian town will have one or two. The expatriate population in your town will probably all use the same person, which means this person will be used to dealing with foreigners, but beware that he or she does not charge over the odds simply because you are a foreigner. If you can, compare the fees of a couple of *commercialisti* to make sure you are paying a reasonable fee.

Fiscal representative

If you are not living in Italy all the time, you may want to consider appointing a fiscal representative. This will probably be a *commercialista* who will undertake all dealings with the tax authorities on your behalf. Alternatively you may want to instruct a bilingual financial adviser in your own country who is familiar with both tax systems.

ICI (Imposta Communali Sugli Immobili)

This is an annual local tax that is determined by the size of the property that you own. It is levied at between 0.4 and 0.7 per cent of the property's cadastral value and is based on the value declared at the land registry.

This tax is payable whether you are resident or non-resident. Many foreigners do not realize that they still have to pay *ICI* even if their house is being restored and is therefore uninhabitable. If you do not pay on time, you will have to pay a fine. *ICI* is paid in two instalments, 50 per cent in June and 50 per cent in December. Non-residents can generally pay in one lump sum.

Wealth tax

There is no wealth tax and inheritance tax has also been abolished. If someone is a resident in Italy he or she is now able to pass assets to their immediate family either during their lifetime or on death, without any liability to gift or estate tax. However, the property will be subject to Italian forced heirship rules. These stipulate that if there is just one spouse and no children, the spouse is automatically entitled to half of the estate. If there is a spouse and one child, a third of the estate goes to each. If there is a spouse and children, a quarter of the estate goes to the spouse and half of the estate to the children. If there is a spouse, no children, but ascendants (parents, grandparents): a quarter of the estate goes to the ascendants and half of the estate to the spouse. If there are only children and no spouse, then half the estate goes to a single child; if there is more than one child two-thirds of the estate goes to the children in equal shares. If there are only ascendants left, a third of the estate goes to the ascendants.

Capital gains tax

Capital gains tax is being phased out and in most cases there is no longer any capital gains tax (*INVIM*) on the sale of land and buildings in Italy, but it is worth taking advice because some people have found that unless they buy another house within two years, they become liable for some form of capital gains tax.

Appeals

If you disagree with the amount of tax that you are required to pay in Italy you can appeal against the decision of the *intendenza di finanza*. Consult a *commercialista* who will assist you through the appeals process.

Conventions for the avoidance of double taxation

Italy has signed a convention with the UK and the USA for the avoidance of double taxation. This convention is also in force in the following countries: Albania, Algeria, Argentina, Australia, Bangladesh, Belgium, Brazil, Bulgaria, Canada, Czechoslovakia, China, Cyprus, South Korea, The Ivory Coast, Denmark, Egypt, The Arab Emirates, Ecuador, Estonia, The Philippines, Finland, France, Germany, Japan, Greece, India, Indonesia, Ireland, Israel, former Yugoslavia, Kazakhstan, Kenya, Kuwait, Lithuania, Luxembourg, Malaysia, Macedonia, Malta, Morocco, Mauritius, Mexico. Norway, New Zealand, The Netherlands, Pakistan, Poland, Portugal, Romania, Russia, Senegal, Singapore, Spain, Sri Lanka, South Africa, Sweden, Switzerland, Tanzania, Thailand, Trinidad and Tobago, Tunisia, Turkey, Hungary, Russia, Venezuela, Vietnam and Zambia.

Postscript

By now you should have a better idea of what is entailed in buying a property in Italy. This basic knowledge of the process will help protect you against the pitfalls facing all prospective buyers in Italy. Armed with this essential information and with sound research on your chosen area, you should soon be on your way to buying the Italian home of your dreams. Remember, if you are in any difficulties at all, it is best to take professional advice.

Ironically, those hoping to simplify their lives by moving to Italy full-time will come to realize that first they have to complicate their lives even more. Buying a house and finding work in Italy, or retiring here, takes time, effort and a steady nerve. But if you are realistic about the challenges ahead, you will find your new life very rewarding.

The author Norman Lewis was one of the great British writers about Italy – his books *Naples '44* and *The Honoured Society* are acknowledged as classics. He wrote, 'Were I given the chance to be born again, Italy would be the country of my choice.' It's hard to disagree with him.

Appendix 1: Useful addresses

Embassies and honorary consulates

The British Embassy
Via XX Settembre, 80a
00187 Rome
Tel: 06 42200001

British Consulate
Via S Paolo, 7
20121 Milan
Tel: 02 723001

British Consulate
Via Saluzzo, 60
10125 Turin
Tel: 011 650 9202

British Consulate
Campo della Carità
Dorsoduro 1051
Venice
Tel: 041 522 7207

British Consulate
Via di Francia, 28
16149 Genoa
Tel: 010 416 828

Appendix 1: Useful Addresses

British Consulate
Via Dante Alighieri, 7
34122 Trieste
Tel: 040 347 8303

British Consulate
Lungarno Corsini, 2
50123 Florence
Tel: 055 284 133
Commercial Section: 055 289556

British Consulate
Viale Colombo, 160
09045 Quartu S. Elena
Cagliari
Tel: 070 828628

British Consulate
Via dei Mille, 40
80121 Naples
Tel: 081 423 8911

British Consulate
Via Dalmazia, 127
70121 Bari
Tel: 080 554 3668

British Consulate
Via Cadorna, 14
98100 Messina
Tel: 090 672924

British Consulate
Via Verdi, 53
95100 Catania
Tel: 095 715 1864

British Consulate
Via Cavour, 121
90133 Palermo
Tel: 091 326412

Other embassies

Australia
Via Alessandria, 215
00198 Rome
Tel: 06 8527 21

Canada
Via GB de Rossi, 27
00161 Rome
Tel: 06 445 981

Denmark
Via dei Monti Parioli, 50
00197 Rome
Tel: 06 320 0441

France
Piazza Farnese, 67
00186 Rome
Tel: 06 68 6011

Germany
Via San Martino della Bataglia, 4
00185 Rome
Tel: 06 492 131

Ireland
Largo Nazareno, 3
00187 Rome
Tel: 06 6782 541

Netherlands
Via Michele Marcati, 8
00197 Rome
Tel: 06 322 1141

New Zealand
Via Zara 28
00198 Rome
Tel: 06 441 7171

South Africa
Via Tanaro, 14
00198 Rome
Tel: 06 852 541

Sweden
Piazza Rio di Janeiro, 3
Casella Postale 7201
00100 Rome
Tel: 06 441941

United States of America
Via Vittorio Veneto, 119a
00187 Rome
Tel: 06 46741

General information on Italy

Italian Embassy
Three Kings Yard
London W1K 4EH
Tel: 020 7312 2200
Web site: www.embitaly.org.uk
See the Embassy's Web site for general information.

Italian Cultural Institute
39 Belgrave Square
London SW1X 8NT
Tel: 020 7325 1461
Web site: www.italcultur.org.uk
The official Italian government agency for promotion of Italian life and culture. Offers language classes for beginners through to advanced level and collaborations between universities and academic societies. Promotes concerts, symposiums and exhibitions.

British Italian Society
The Offices of Venice in Peril Fund
5th floor, Stamford Bridge
Fulham Road
London SW6 1HS
Tel: 020 7924 6883 (Monday and Tuesday each week, plus answerphone)
Web site: www.british-italian.org
This organization has been promoting friendship between Britain and the UK for 60 years. Promotes concerts, exhibitions, food tastings, etc.

Italian State Tourist Board
1 Princes Street
London W1B 2AY
Tel: 020 7408 1254
Web site: www.enit.it

Italian Chamber of Commerce
1 Princes Street
London W1B 2AY
Tel: 020 7495 8191
Web site: www.italchamind.org.uk

Italian Trade Commission
37 Sackville Street
London W1S 3DQ
Tel: 020 7734 2412
Web site: www.italtrade.com

Appendix 1: Useful Addresses

British Chamber of Commerce in Italy
Via Dante 12, 20121 Milan
Tel: +39 02 877798 (Milan)
Web site: www.britchamitaly.com
Private, non-profit-making organization that helps entrepreneurs, small businesses and other companies to become established in Italy. Provides business support and useful contacts.

The British Council
Via Manzoni 38, 20121 Milan
Web site: www.britishcouncil.it
Has information on equivalence of qualifications and other educational enquiries.

Department for Work and Pensions Benefits Agency
Overseas Division Medical Benefits
Tyneview Park
Whitley Road
Newcastle upon Tyne NE98 1BA
Tel: 0191 218 7547
Hours of business: Monday to Friday 8am to 4pm.
   If you have an industrial injury or occupational disease, and intend taking up residence in Italy, special rules apply. Please write to the above address and include the words 'Industrial Injuries Section, Room TC013', or telephone: 0191 218 7650/1.

Department of Health
International Branch
Room 542A
Richmond House
79 Whitehall
London SW1A 2NS
Tel: 020 7210 4850

Inland Revenue
National Insurance Contributions Office
International Services
Benton Park View
Newcastle upon Tyne NE98 1ZZ
Tel: 0845 915 4811
From Italy: 00 44 191 225 4811

Useful Web site addresses

www.esteri.it
Italian Ministry of Foreign Affairs

www.englishyellowpages.it
The English Yellow Pages

www.paginegialle.it
The Italian Yellow Pages

www.paginebianche.it
The Italian Telephone Directory

www.istruzione.it
The Italian Ministry of Education in Rome

www.mincomes.it
Ministry of Foreign Trade in Rome

www.ecis.org
European Council of International Schools

www.istruzione.it
Information on school registration

www.finanze.it
Information on Italian taxes; tax form downloadable

Useful numbers

Benvenuto Club, Milan
Links to other expat clubs
www.benvenutomilano.net

Alcoholics Anonymous
Tel: 06 4742913

Narcotics Anonymous
Tel: 06 860 4788

The Samaritans
Tel: 06 704 54444

British Labour Party in Rome
Tel: 06 509 12326

Commonwealth Club
06 844 82745

Circolo di cultura Mario Mieli
Gay and lesbian support group
Tel: 06 541 3985

Professional Women's Association
Tel: 06 582 7657

Teacher Information Exchange and Support (TIES)
Tel: 06 957 6131

Religion

Details of churches in Italy other than Catholic churches can be found from the British Consulates. For Anglican services, call 06 3600 1881. For the International Christian Fellowship call 06 482 5865. The Society of Friends (Quakers) can be contacted on 06 397 45760.

St Andrew's Presbyterian Church is in Via XX Settembre 7, Rome, Tel: 06 482 7627. Italy's main Islamic Mosque is also in Rome at Via della Moschea, Tel: 06 808 2167. The Buddhist Vihara is at Via Mandas 2, Rome, Tel: 06 224 60091.

Airlines

British Airways
Tel: 0845 773 3377
Web site: www.britishairways.com

Alitalia
Tel: 0870 544 8259
Web site: www.alitalia.co.uk

Ryanair
Tel: 0871 246 0000
Web site: www.ryanair.com

easyJet
Tel: 0870 600 0000
Web site: www.easyjet.co.uk

Meridiana
Tel: 020 7839 2222
Web site: www.meridiana.it (English version available)

BMI Baby
Tel: 0870 607 0555
Web site: www.flybmi.com

MyTravelLite
Tel: 0870 1564564
Web site: www.mytravellite.com

Air One
Tel: 06 488 800 (Rome)
Web site: www.flyairone.it

Britannia Airways
Tel: 0870 607 6757
Web site: www.britanniaairways.com

FlyGlobespan
Tel: 08705 561 522
Web site: www.flyglobespan.com

Aer Lingus
Tel: 0845 084 4444
Web site: www.aerlingus.com

Air 2000
Tel: 0870 757 2757
Web site: http://air2000.com

Monarch Airlines
Tel: 08700 40 50 40
Web site: www.monarch-airlines.com

Volare
Tel: 00 800 454 000 00 (from outside Italy) or 800 454 000 (from Italy)
Web site: www.volareweb.com

Duo Airlines
Tel: 0871 700 0700
Web site: www.duo.com

Rail

Eurotunnel
Tel: 0870 535 3535
Web site: www.eurotunnel.com

Rail Europe
Tel: 0870 584 8848
Web site: www.raileurope.com

Italian State Railways
Tel: (in Italy, with no dialling prefix) 892021
Web site: www.trenitalia.it

Ferries

Hoverspeed
Tel: 0870 240 6070
Web site: www.hoverspeed.com

P&O Ferries
Tel: 0870 600 0611
Web site: www.posl.com

Brittany Ferries
Tel: 0870 556 1600
Web site: www.brittany-ferries.com

Corsica/Sardinia Ferries
UK agents: Viamare Travel, London
Tel: 020 7431 4560.
Web site: www.corsicaferries.com

Tirrenia Ferries
UK agents: SMS UK Travel, London
Tel: 020 7244 8422
Web site: www. gruppotirrenia.it

Ports and harbours in Italy

Augusta in Sicily, Bagnoli, Bari, Brindisi, Gela, Genoa, La Spezia, Livorno, Milazzo, Naples, Porto Foxi, Porto Torres in Sardinia, Salerno, Savona, Tara Trieste, Venice.

Road and route planning

AA
Web site: www.theaa.com

RAC
Web site: www.rac.co.uk

Mappy
Web site: www.mappy.com

Automobile Club Italiano
Web site: www.aci.it

Autostrada information
Web site: www.autostrade.it

Removal firms

All household and personal effects can be transferred duty and tax free from within the EU to Italy provided they are goods that have been owned and used in a previous home. They must be imported within six months of the official transfer of residence. Below is a list of some of the movers that transport personal effects to Italy.

Allied Pickfords (UK)
Tel: 0800 289 229

Baxter Moving Excellence
Tel: 01296 393396
Web site: www.baxter.eu.com

Britannia Bradshaw International
Tel: 0161 946 0809
Web site: www.bradshawinternational.com

Overs International
Tel: 0800 243433
Web site: www.overs.co.uk

For smaller loads you may want to investigate the private removers who advertise in expatriate magazines such as *Wanted in Rome* (www.wantedinrome.com) and *The Informer* online magazine (www.informer.it), but check that the person you are dealing with has adequate insurance.

English language resources

The Informer – this online magazine is packed with useful information on all the issues involved in living and working in Italy. Some of the information is available free, for the rest you must pay a subscription. It is very good value for money – you can access archive material, it keeps you up to date with the latest news affecting foreigners in Italy and answers questions about tax deadlines, etc. A serious and comprehensive resource for incomers to Italy. Web site: www.informer.it.

Wanted in Rome – a fortnightly magazine with information on rented accommodation, jobs and local events in the capital city. Web site: www.wantedinrome.com.

Grapevine – a monthly magazine for the residents of Lucca in Tuscany, written in English. Web site: www.luccagrapevine.com.

Easy Milano – a fortnightly publication distributed in 120 pick-up points. Articles on all aspects of life in Milan and Italy, as well as job adverts and accommodation for rent. Web site: www.easymilano.it.

The Web site www.italyweekly.it was a partnership between the *International Herald Tribune* and *Corriere della Sera* but is now longer active. However, you can still view the useful information that remains on the site. This includes a list of all the universities in Italy and their contact addresses.

www.insight-italy.com. Run by expatriate Helen Burgess who offers cultural awareness training for businesspeople and relocation and integration services in Italy.

English language cinemas in Italy

Florence: Odeon
Rome: Metropolitan and Pasquino
Milan: Anteo, Arcobaleno, Mexico and Odeon

Satellite TV

Eurosat – distribution, installation and servicing of satellite TV systems. For list of local providers contact eursat@libero.it.

English language bookshops and libraries

The Almost Corner Bookshop
Via del Moro 45
Trastevere
Rome
Tel: 06 583 6942
Open Sundays

Anglo American Bookstore
Via della Vite 102 (near the Spanish Steps)
Rome
Tel: 06 679 5222
Open Tuesdays to Saturdays non-stop. Closed Monday mornings.
Web site: www.aab.it

British Council Library
Via delle Quattro Fontane 20
Rome
Tel: 06 478141
Open Mon, Tues, Thurs, Fri 10am till 5pm. Open Weds noon till 5pm.
Open Sat 10.30am till 12.30pm.

La Piccola Libreria
Via Marconi
Paciano
Perugia

Da Pilade
Via delle Ruote 22r
Florence 50129
Tel: 055 46 33 042

BM Book Shop
Borgo Ognissanti 4r
Florence

Armani superstore
Via Manzoni 31
Milan
Small international bookshop attached.

Panton's English Bookshop
Via Masceroni, 12
Milan
Tel: 02469 4468
E-mail: info@englishbookshop.it

Rental agencies

Property International
Rome office – Tel: 06 574 3170
Milan office – Tel: 02 49 80092
Web site: www.propertyint.net

Dimensione Casufficio
Palazzo Colonna
Apostoli 66
Rome
Tel: 06 6994 1681

Legal advice

John Howell and Co
22 Endell Street
London WC2 9AD
Tel: 020 7420 0400
e-mail: info@europelaw.com
Web site: www.europelaw.com

Claudio Del Giudice
Rivington House
82 Great Eastern Street
London EC2A 3JF
Tel: 020 7613 2788
e-mail: delgiudice@clara.co.uk
Web site: www.delgiudice.clara.net

Roberto Barbalich
Studio Legale
2999 San Polo
30125 Venice
Tel: 00 39 041 714 570
e-mail: barbalichr@tin.it

Sarah Panizzo
Penningtons Solicitors
Bucklersbury House
83 Cannon Street
London EC4N 8PE
Tel: 020 7457 3000

Estate agents

Andrea Cristofanelli Broglio
Tel: 00 39 389 0215 833
e-mail: andcb@tin.it
Web site: www.marchecountry.com

Danny Beattie
Open Door Italia Ltd
Tel: 00 30 0737 630545 or 00 39 339 8920567
e-mail: posthouse@libero it
No Web site; works in Marche through personal referrals.

Euro Property
Tel: 00 39 844 397
Web site: www.europropertynet.com

Chianti Estates
Managing Director Bill Thomson
Tel: 00 39 0577 731120
Web site: www.knightfrank.com

Diana Levins Moore
Tel: 00 39 0578 268016
e-mail: levinsmoore@bcc.tin.it
Web site: Tuscany-Inside-Out.com

Financial advisers

Robin Vos
Macfarlanes
10 Norwich Street
London EC4A 1BD
Tel: 020 7831 92222
Web site: www.macfarlanes.com

Bompani Audit
Piazza D'Azeglio 39
Firenze 50121
Tel: 055 247 7851
e-mail: ba.firenze@mri-bompaniaudit.com
(Offices all over Italy)

Moores Rowland International
3 Sheldon Square
London W2 6PS
Tel: 020 7470 0000
Web site: http://www.mrilondon.com

Roberto Barbalich
Studio Legale
2999 San Polo
30125 Venice
Tel: 00 39 041 714 570
e-mail: barbalichr@tin.it

Sarah Panizzo
Penningtons Solicitors
Bucklersbury House
83 Cannon Street
London EC4N 8PE
Tel: 020 7457 3000

Banks, etc

Intesa BCI
90 Queen Street
London EC4 1SA
Tel: 020 7651 3000

Banca Nazionale Del Lavoro
Fitzwilliam House
10 St Mary Axe
London EC3A 8NA
Tel: 020 7337 2400

Banca Monte Dei Paschi Di Siena
122 Leadenhall Street
London EC3V 4RH
Tel: 020 7645 7800

Banca Di Roma
Guildhall House
81–87 Gresham Street
London EC2V 7NQ
Tel: 020 7726 4106

UniCredito Italiano
17 Moorgate
London EC2R 6PH
Tel: 020 7606 9011

Banca San Paolo IMI
Wren House
15 Carter Lane
London EC4V 5SP
Tel: 020 7214 8000

Appendix 1: Useful Addresses

Banca D'Italia
39 King Street
London EC2V 8JJ
Tel: 020 7606 4201

Woolwich Europe Ltd
Watling Street
Bexleyheath
Kent DA6 7RR
Tel: 0800 33 44 99

Conti Financial Services
204 Church Road
Hove
East Sussex BN3 2DJ
Tel: 01273 772 811

Appendix 2:
Direct flights to Italy from the UK

(S = Summer only)

To	From	Airline
Alghero	London Stansted	Ryanair
	Manchester	(S) BA
Ancona	London Stansted	Ryanair
Bari	London Stansted	Ryanair
	London Gatwick	BA
Bologna	London Gatwick	BA
Bologna (Forli)	London Stansted	Ryanair, easyJet
Brescia	London Gatwick	(S) Monarch
	Bristol	(S) Charter
Cagliari	Luton	Air Volare
	London Gatwick	BA
Catania	London Gatwick	(S) Charter
	Manchester	(S) BMI; MyTravel; T Cook
Florence	London Gatwick	Alitalia
Genoa	London Gatwick	BA
	London Stansted	Ryanair
Milan Bergamo	Cardiff	BMI Baby
	Glasgow-Prestwick	Ryanair
	London Stansted	Ryanair
Milan Linate	London Heathrow	BA, BMI, Alitalia
	London Gatwick	easyJet
	London Stansted	easyJet
Milan Malpensa	Birmingham	BA, FlyBe
	Cork	Aer Lingus
	Dublin	Aer Lingus, Alitalia,
	East Midlands	BMI Baby
	Edinburgh	Duo Airlines

Appendix 2: Direct Flights to Italy from the UK

To	From	Airline
	Leeds/Bradford	Channel Express
	London Heathrow	BA, Alitalia
	Manchester	(S) BA, Charter, Alitalia
	Southampton	FlyBe
Naples	Birmingham	(S) Britannia, Air 2000
	Bristol	(S) Britannia, Air 2000
	East Midlands	(S) Air 2000
	Glasgow	(S) Britannia
	London Stansted	easyJet
	London Gatwick	BA, (S) Britannia, Air 2000, Monarch
	Luton	(S) Britannia
	Manchester	(S) Air 2000, Britannia
Olbia	London Gatwick	Meridiana
Palermo	London Gatwick	(S) Monarch
	London Stansted	Ryanair
	Luton	(S) Monarch
Pescara	London Stansted	Ryanair
Pisa	Birmingham	MyTravel
	Bristol	(S) Charter
	East Midlands	BMI Baby
	Leeds/Bradford	(S) Charter
	London Stansted	Ryanair
	London Gatwick	BA, (S) Air 2000, Monarch
	Manchester	BA, (S) Britannia, Air 2000
Rimini	London Stansted	(S) Charter
	Manchester	(S) MyTravel
Rome (Ciampino)	London Stansted	Ryanair, easyJet
	Edinburgh	(S) FlyGlobespan
	Glasgow	(S) FlyGlobespan
Rome (Fiumicino)	Birmingham	BA
	Cork	Aer Lingus
	Dublin	Alitalia
	Edinburgh	(S) BA
	London Gatwick	BA, Alitalia
	London Heathrow	BA, Alitalia
	Manchester	BA
Trieste	London Stansted	Ryanair
Turin	London Gatwick	(S) Air 2000
	London Stansted	Ryanair
	Manchester	(S) Air 2000

To	From	Airline
Venice (Marco Polo)	Bristol	easyJet, (S) Charter
	Birmingham	BA, BMI Baby, (S) Monarch
	Dublin	Aer Lingus
	East Midlands	easyJet
	London Gatwick	BA, (S) Monarch
	London Heathrow	BMI
	London Stansted	easyJet, Ryanair
	Manchester	BA, (S) Britannia, Astraeus, Monarch, MyTravel
Venice (Treviso)	London Stansted	Ryanair
Verona	Bristol	(S) Charter
	Leeds/Bradford	(S) Charter
	London Gatwick	BA
	London Stansted	Ryanair
	Manchester	(S) BA, Britannia, Excel

Appendix 3: Useful vocabulary

Purchasing terminology

acquirente	buyer
affitare	to rent
annullare un contratto	to cancel a contract
caparra	deposit
catasto	land map registry
certificato	certificate
clausola condizionale	special condition
comprare, acquistare	to buy
compravendita, rogito or *atto di acquisto*	the final contract that seals the sale
compromesso	the written document that details what you are going to buy (land, property and contents)
comproprietà	joint ownership
condizioni di vendita	conditions of sale
diritto di accesso, diritto di passaggio	right of way
honorario, parcella	fee
atto di proprietà	title deed
licenza edilizia	planning permission
particella	parcel of land
la pratica	conveyancing

prelazioni	pre-emption rights (the right of a neighbour who makes most of his living from farming to buy the property and land)
rogito or atto	transfer of title from the vendor to buyer
venditore	seller
spese	costs
testamento	will
trattabile	negotiable
vendere	to sell

Types of property

appartamento	flat
appartamento su due piani	maisonette
azienda agricola, fattoria	farm
casa colonica, casa rustica	farmhouse
casa in rovina	ruined house
casa padronale	country house
castello	castle
chiesa sconsacrata	deconsecrated church
fabbricato rurale	rural building
fienile, granaio, stalla	barn
monolocale	studio flat
palazzo	large building
torre	tower
villa	detached house
villetta	small detached house
rustico	farm building

Property details

abitabile	habitable
alberi	trees
aria condizionaria	air conditioning
attaccate	joined (to another property)

bagno	bathroom
balcone, terrazzo	balcony
bosco	wood
buona posizione	in a good position
caldaia	boiler
camera da letto	bedroom
caminetto, focolare	fireplace
camino	chimney
in campagna	in the countryside
campo	field
cancello	gate
cantina	cellar or storage
centralissima	very central position
in centro	in town
cisterna	water tank
corridoio	corridor
in corso di costruzione	being built
cortile	courtyard
cucina	kitchen
da ristrutturare	to restore
finestre	windows
fiume	river
fossa biologica, fossa settica	septic tank
fronte mare	facing the sea
giardino	garden
ingresso	entrance hall
interrato	basement
lavanderia	laundry room
al mare	by the sea
nella citta	in the city
ottimo stato	in excellent condition
parcheggio, posto auto	parking space
parete, muro	wall
pavimento	floor
persiane	shutters
piano	storey
piscina	swimming pool
porta	door

pozzo	well
recinto	paddock
recinzione	fencing
riscaldamento	central heating
ruscello	stream
sala, stanza	room
scala	staircase
scaldaacqua, scaldabagno	water heater
soffitta	loft
soggiorno	living room
spiaggia	beach
strada bianca	road without tarmac
strada comunale	road accessible to all members of the community
strada privata	private road
strada vicinale	road for, and usually maintained by, local inhabitants
tetto	roof
uliveto	olive grove
vista mare	sea view
vista montagne	mountain view

Useful terms for renovation

altezza	height
cantiere	building site
coppi	roof tiles
costruire	to build
demolizione	demolition
disegno in scala	scale drawing
gronda	gutter
incassato	built-in
largezza	width
lunghezza	length
mattoni/pietra a vista	exposed brickwork/stonework
offerta di appalto	tender for work

perizia	survey
portone	exterior doors
preventivo	estimate
profoundità	depth
restauro	renovation
scavo	excavation
stuccare	to re-point
telaio di finestra	window frame
trave	roof beam

Plumbing

bidet	bidet
box doccia	shower unit
gabinetto	toilet
guarnizione	washer
lavandino	sink
perdita, fuoriuscita, infiltrazione	leak
riscaldamento	heating
rubinetti	taps
sifone	u-bend
tubi di scarico	waste pipes
tubo	pipe
vasca	bath

Useful people

agente immobiliare	estate agent
architetto	architect
avvocato	lawyer
capo	boss
commercialista	accountant
elettricista	electrician
falegname	carpenter

geometra	surveyor, project manager
giardiniere	gardener
idraulico	plumber
imbianchino	painter
impresa edile	building contractor
ingegnere	engineer
muratore	mason, bricklayer
notaio	notary
operai	general building workers
pavimentista	floor tile layer
sindaco	mayor

Building materials

acciaio	steel
acqua	water
breccia	gravel
calcio	lime
cartongesso	plasterboard
cemento	cement
colla	glue
cotto	terracotta tiles
ferro	iron
intonaco	plaster
isolante	insulation
legno	wood
malta	grout
marmo	marble
mattone	brick
mattonelle	small bricks or tiles
pietra	stone
sabbia	sand
specchio	mirror
vernice, tinta	paint
vetro	glass

Tools

cacciavite	screwdriver
chiave	spanner, or wrench
chiodi	nails
livello	spirit level
martello	hammer
metro	tape measure
pala	shovel
punta	drill bit
sabbiatrice	sandblaster
scalpello	chisel
sega	saw
trapano	drill
vite	screws

Dealing with the authorities

anagrafe	bureau of statistics or census office
certificato di assicurazione	insurance certificate
certificato di nascita, di morte, di matrimonio, di cittadinanza	birth, death, marriage, citizenship certificate
certificato di residenza	residence permit
codice fiscale	individual fiscal number, similar to the British national insurance number
comune	town hall, local authority
intendenza di finanza	tax office
libretto di lavoro	work registration card
passaporto	passport
patente di guida	driving licence
permesso di soggiorno	permit to stay
stato di famiglia	family status documents

Financial

al lordo delle tasse	before tax
anno fiscale	tax year
banca	bank
bancomat	cash machine
cassa di risparmio	savings bank
cassiere	bank teller
conto corrente	current account
contribuente	tax payer
costituire una società	to form a company
debito	debt
detraibile dalle imposte	tax-deductible
detrazione d'imposta	tax allowance
il direttore	bank manager
dichiarazione fiscale	tax return
esenzione fiscale	tax exemption
evasione fiscale	tax evasion
fisco	the taxman
gestore	account manager
mandato di pagamento	
permanente	standing order
imponibile	taxable
Imposta Communale sugli	
Immobili (ICI)	municipal or local property tax
Imposta di Registro	registration tax
Imposta sul reddito delle	
persone fisiche (IRPEF)	personal income tax, changing to IRE
Imposta sul valore	
aggiunto (IVA)	value added tax (VAT)
imposte incluse	including tax
ipoteca	mortgage
libretto di assegni	cheque book
movimenti	bank account details
netto delle tasse	after tax
mutuo	mortgage loan
pagare a saldo	pay in full

plusvalenza	capital gain
prelevare	to withdraw (money)
prestito	loan
ragioniere/commercialista	accountant
rimborso fiscale	tax rebate
saldo	the balance of an account
saldo attivo	credit
saldo passivo	deficit
scoperto (di conto)	overdraft
sgravio fiscale	tax relief
Società in Accomandita Semplice (SAS)	limited partnership
Società in Nome Colletivo (SNC)	unlimited partnership
Società per Azioni (SpA)	joint-stock company
Società Responsibilita Limitata (SRL)	limited company
spese istruttoria	mortgage arrangement fees
sportello	bank counter
tassazione	taxation
tasso di cambio	rate of exchange
tasso d'interesse	interest rate
versare	to deposit (money)

Medical

allergia	allergy
allergico	allergic
ambulatorio	surgery
azienda sanitaria locale ASL, unità sanitaria locale USL	local health authority
cassa	cashier
clinico	private hospital or clinic
consultorio familiare	local health centre
farmacia	pharmacy
frattura	fracture

ictus	stroke
impegnativa	medical referral
infarto	heart attack
medico, dottore	doctor
ospedale	hospital
pronto soccorso	casualty department
ricetta	prescription
rotto/a	broken
sangue	blood
Servizio Sanitario	
Nazionale SSN	national health service
tessera sanitaria	health card
ticket	flat-rate prescription/charge
ufficio straniero	immigration office

Cars

benzina	petrol
bollo auto	car tax
Codice della Strada	Highway Code
libretto	logbook, ownership document for car
patente	licence
pieno	full tank
targa nazionale	number plate

Utilities

abbonamento	standing charge
bolletta	bill
consumo calcolato	estimated consumption
contatore	meter
data di scadenza	pay-by date
fattura	receipt
riepilogo dei costi	summary of costs
scato del contatore	kilowatt hour

segnalare un guasto	to report a breakdown of service
totale da pagare	total to be paid

Internet

allegato	attachment
avanti	next
chiocciola	name for @ symbol
collegamento	link
e-mail	e-mail/e-mail address
esci	exit
indietro	previous, back
inviare un messaggio	to send an e-mail
motore di ricerca	search engine
password	password
punto	dot
rete	network
schermo	screen
sito web	Web site
trasferire	download
tratto	hyphen

Appendix 4:
Universities in the UK where Italian is taught

University of Aberystwyth
Web site: www.aber.ac.uk, Tel: 01970 623111

Anglia Polytechnic University
Web site: www.anglia.ac.uk, Tel: 01223 363271

University of Bangor
Web site: www.bangor.ac.uk, Tel: 01248 351151

University of Bath
Web site: www.bath.ac.uk, Tel: 01225 388388

University of Birmingham
Web site: www.birmingham.ac.uk, Tel: 0121 414 3344

Queen's University Belfast
Web site: www.qub.ac.uk, Tel: 02980 245 133

University of Bristol
Web site: www.bristol.ac.uk, Tel: 0117 928 9000

University of Cambridge
Web site: www.cam.ac.uk, Tel: 01223 337733

Appendix 4: UK Universities Teaching Italian

University of Durham
Web site: www.durham.ac.uk, Tel: 0191 334 2000

University of Edinburgh
Web site: www.edinburgh.ac.uk, Tel: 0131 650 1000

University of Essex
Web site: www.essex.ac.uk, Tel: 01206 873333

University of Exeter
Web site: www.exeter.ac.uk, Tel: 01392 661000

University of Glasgow
Web site: www.glasgow.ac.uk, Tel: 0141 330 2000

University of Hull
Web site: www.hull.ac.uk, Tel: 01482 346311

University of Kent
Web site: www.kent.ac.uk, Tel: 01 227 764000

University of Leeds
Web site: www.leeds.ac.uk, Tel: 0113 243 1751

University of Leicester
Web site: www.leicester.ac.uk, Tel: 0116 252 2522

University College, London
Web site: www.ucl.ac.uk, Tel: 020 7679 2000

Royal Holloway, University of London
Web site: www.rhul.ac.uk, Tel: 01784 434455

University of Manchester
Web site: www.manchester.ac.uk, Tel: 0161 275 2000

Manchester Metropolitan University
Web site: www.mmu.ac.uk, Tel: 0161 247 2000

Oxford Brookes University
Web site: www.brookes.ac.uk, Tel: 01865 741111

University of Reading
Web site: www.reading.ac.uk, Tel: 0118 987 5123

University of St Andrews
Web site: www.st-and.ac.uk, Tel: 01334 476161

University of Strathclyde
Web site: www.strathclyde.ac.uk, Tel: 0141 552 4400

University of Sussex (Brighton)
Web site: www.sussex.ac.uk, Tel: 01273 606755

University of Swansea
Web site: www. swansea.ac.uk, Tel: 01792 205678

University of Warwick
Web site: www.warwick.ac.uk, Tel: 024 7652 3523

University of Westminster
Web site: www.westminster.ac.uk, Tel: 020 7911 5000

Appendix 5:
Italian public holidays

January 1 – New Year's Day
January 6 – Epiphany
April 12 – Easter Monday (in 2004)
April 25 – Liberation Day
May 1 – May Day
June 2 – anniversary of the founding of the Republic
August 15 – Assumption Day, also known as *Ferragosto*
November 1 – All Saints' Day
December 8 – Immaculate Conception
December 25 – Christmas Day
December 26 – St Stephen's Day

On public holidays in Italy many museums and art galleries close or have shorter opening hours. Public transport services may also be limited. Restaurants and shops are generally closed.

Each town also celebrates its own saint's day when local facilities may close.

Appendix 6:
Pet travel arrangements

The Department For Environment Food and Rural Affairs (DEFRA) has approved a number of ferry companies and one rail company that are now taking bookings to carry pets to and from the UK. Direct air routes from Italy have also been approved. The documentary and microchip checks will be carried out by the ferry companies, the airlines or the train operators, under UK government supervision. The approved companies are as follows.

By sea

(With a vehicle, unless otherwise shown)

Calais to Dover: Hoverspeed*, P&O Stena or Sea France
Cherbourg or Le Havre to Portsmouth: P&O Portsmouth*
Caen or St Malo to Portsmouth: Britanny Ferries
Cherbourg to Poole: Britanny Ferries
Ostend to Dover: Hoverspeed*
Roscoff or Santander to Plymouth: Britanny Ferries

*May accept pets with foot passengers, check with the company.

By rail

Calais (Coquelles) to Folkestone (Cheriton): Eurotunnel Shuttle Service (ie, with a vehicle only. Please note: the Eurostar passenger train service from Paris or Brussels cannot be used).

By air

Because of frequent changes to the flights from Italy accepting pets, you should check first on the DEFRA Web site (www.defra.gov.uk) for updated information. Airlines usually require dogs or cats to travel in the aircraft's hold.

Pet-owners from other countries who wish to travel back and forth to Italy should consult their embassies for advice.

Appendix 7:
Miscellaneous information

Hazards of nature

Italy is prone to various hazards of nature, earthquakes and volcanic eruptions being the best-known dangers. The Italian National Seismic Network records an estimated 2,000 earthquakes a year, although most are so small as to be undetectable. The highest seismic risk is in Sicily, Calabria, Friuli-Venezia Guilia, Campania and Marche while the rest of the country has a low to medium risk. Puglia and Sardinia are relatively aseismic. Mount Etna last erupted in 1998 and has been active ever since while in 1983–5, 36,000 people had to be relocated from their homes when Mount Vesuvius was 'uplifted' by seismic disturbances.

Many homes in Italy, including my own, are not earthquake-proof but all public buildings such as apartment blocks, schools, etc, in areas of known risk must now be built to earthquake-resistant standards. When we questioned our *geometra* about whether or not this should be done, he pointed out that our house had been left unscathed through the earthquakes of the last 100 years or so and that it was obviously solid enough as it is.

Other regional risks include landslides, mudflows and flooding – largely because of Italy's weather system, which can mean hot, dry summers followed by periods of intensive rain.

Hunting

If you live in the Italian countryside you are likely to come across hunters – squads of up to 50 men in camouflage gear, striding through the olive groves with their shotguns and walkie-talkies and with packs of dogs yelping at their feet. Trespass is not a concept the Italians are familiar with and most rural land is accessible to hunters and ramblers, so you will almost certainly see people on your land throughout the year and especially in the autumn and winter months. The hunting season lasts from September until 31 January and during that time hunters are free to shoot *cinghiale* (wild boar), *lepre* (hare), *daino* (deer) and birds. *Fagiano* (pheasant), *faraona* (guinea fowl) and little birds like *tordi* (thrushes) and *allodole* (larks) will end up roasted in the pot or grilled on skewers. Each region has its own rules but in my part of Umbria hunters are allowed to shoot *cinghiale* three days a week – Saturdays, Sundays and Thursdays. On Tuesdays and Fridays they can shoot other animals and birds, leaving two days without any hunting activity. Italian law states that all hunters must be over the age of 18 and have to pass a written exam before they are allowed to use a gun. No one is allowed to drink alcohol on a shoot.

Hunters are not supposed to walk through gardens, vegetable plots and fields of crops and they should stay well away from your house. It is easier to keep hunters at a distance if your property is fenced in, but many Italian houses are in open countryside therefore in practice this is not always viable. If you do find hunters too near your house, ask them politely but firmly to move away. Usually they will do so. Try not to get into a shouting match: it is best to just let them move on and go about their business. Most hunters are law-abiding and very pleasant to deal with, but I have heard of resentful hunters laying down poison for family dogs and ripping up barriers that are in their way, so it doesn't do to provoke them.

In some parts of Italy wild boar have been imported from Hungary and let loose in the countryside to boost the number of animals available for hunting, so the *cinghiale* that you buy at the butchers' shop or that is served in restaurants may come from Hungarian stock.

Hornets

During the summer you may be pestered by hornets (*calabrone*).We were fed up being dive-bombed by these vicious creatures, which were nesting in a tree in our garden somewhere, and bought glass insect traps in the hope of solving the problem. One of our Italian neighbours challenged us to a race – our expensive glass bottles against his homemade insect trap fashioned out of an ordinary plastic mineral water bottle. Within a week, Roberto's bottle was filled with dozens of dead hornets while our elegant glass bottles were still completely empty. We don't know why it works so well, but we have used his method ever since and have never been bothered by hornets again. I don't feel guilty about killing hornets since a sting can be dangerous. In our neighbourhood a doctor in his forties collapsed and died after being stung by a hornet, so everyone is very cautious now.

To make a hornet trap – take a plastic water bottle and cut off the top about three-quarters of the way up. Discard the bottle top. Invert the smaller part and fit it into the lower part of the bottle. Make two holes in the side so that the bottle can be hung from a tree. Fill the trap with stale beer or sugared water, smear some jam on the outside and put it near a dining table or where you think there may be a hornet nest. The hornets are attracted to the jam, make their way inside the bottle and cannot get out again. Replace the bottle every few days. Do not smear honey on the outside of the bottle trap since it is not good for bees.

Scorpions

The most common ways of being stung by *scorpioni* is putting on your shoe and not noticing that one of the little critters is inside, or by dislodging their hiding place by moving a pile of stones with your bare hands. The golden rule, therefore, is to always shake out your footwear and to use protective gloves in the garden. Scorpion stings are painful but not dangerous and the effects will disappear after an hour or so.

Vipers

Distinguishable from other snakes by their triangular-shaped heads, vipers live under rocks or piles of stones. Use protective gloves in the garden and do not walk in long grass without boots. Vipers like cool, damp places – we once found a large one near our dripping irrigation system and it was dispatched with a shovel amid much shrieking. If a person is bitten, or suspects he or she has been bitten by a viper, go immediately to hospital. An anti-viper vaccine can be bought in pharmacies and stored in the fridge in case your dog or cat is bitten. Take it with you while out on walks, and inject it immediately if your animal is bitten and consult a vet.

House rules

One of the great pleasures of having a house in Italy is having friends to stay, but there is a saying: *'un amico in casa e come un pesce, dopo un po' puzza'*. The translation is: 'a friend in the house is like a fish, after a while it stinks'. This might sound inhospitable, but most people who have holiday homes will tell you that the optimum time for having friends to stay is three nights. Everyone has a good time, but it is not so long that people begin to get bored or get on each other's nerves. Another good house rule is to insist that your guests hire a car so that they will not be dependent on you to run them around. You will have seen Siena, Florence or Palermo 20 times already – give your friends maps and guidebooks and encourage them to go sightseeing without you. You can put your feet up while they're gone!

In the peak summer season, leave a few days between one group of guests going and another arriving or, as Peter Mayle says in his book *A Year in Provence*, you will feel like you are running a small but unprofitable hotel. When guests arrive, warn them about the idiosyncrasies of your house. Tell them they cannot leave lights blazing or your electricity will be cut off. Threaten death to anyone who throws stuff down the loo and blocks up your septic tank – on second thoughts, tell them that they will have to clear up the mess. That is worse than death. Request that everyone pitches in with the cooking and cleaning.

If you want to be a good guest, make your own breakfast and don't greet your hosts with: 'So what are we going to do today?' Have your own plans, clear out every now and then and give your hosts some space. If you are the kind of person who wants to sleep in till noon, you should be in a hotel. It is very irritating to have someone snoring along the corridor while everyone else is up and dressed. If you bring children, do not assume that your hosts find them as fascinating as you do. Late nights at the dinner table are for adults – put the kids to bed or send them off to read books, play games or watch TV elsewhere in the house.

Rubbish

When you buy your wonderful, old deserted farmhouse in the Italian countryside, a nasty surprise may await you. You may find, as we did, that your land has been used as a dumping ground by generations of Italian peasants. Since there were no municipal rubbish collections in the old days, *contadini* who lived in these properties were accustomed to throwing all household detritus over a wall, down into a valley or chucking it out at the bottom of the garden. In the past two years we have cleared huge amounts of rubbish from our land, half-hidden by leaves, soil and fallen trees. Bottles, plastic, china, old shoes and clothes, children's toys, wire netting, old farm implements – we even found a car seat, a bit of a fridge and an ancient television aerial. This is a nasty but necessary job that you may have to tackle. It is something you could do while the builders are working inside the house.

Talking with your hands

Italians gesticulate a lot, using their hands or the expression on their faces to make their point. Here are a few of the gestures that you will come across and what they mean:

▌ The index finger and thumb are joined together in a circle with the other fingers pointing upwards. The hand may be moved for emphasis. Meaning: excellent, I approve.

▌ Both palms held flat, upright and held in front of the face. Meaning: stop, it's not my business.

▌ One palm, held flat and upright. Meaning; stop, the person does not want to hear any more.

▌ The thumb is drawn across the cheek from ear to mouth. Meaning: the person under discussion is cunning and is not to be trusted.

▌ The index finger and thumb are elongated while the other fingers are clasped to the palm. The hand may be moved for emphasis. Meaning: I don't know, I'm not sure.

▌ The fingertips of the hand are brought together and the hand is pointed towards the chin and shaken for emphasis. Meaning: I don't care.

▮ The hand, palm downward, makes a cutting gesture across the throat. Meaning: some kind of threat, not necessarily physical. Some project or a friendship is finished.

▮ A hand held flat across the chest. Meaning: a promise or word of honour.

▮ The fingertips of one hand are put together and the hand is shaken for emphasis. Meaning: impatience with the situation or topic under discussion.

Appendix 8:
Recommended reading

These are some of the books that I have found useful and enjoyed reading about life in Italy.

Living and Working in Italy (2003) edited by Graeme Chesters, Survival Books Ltd, 1st Floor, 60 St James Street, London SW1A 1ZN.

Restoring a Home in Italy: 22 Home-Owners Realize Their Dream, by Elizabeth Minchilli, published by Partisan, USA.

The Essentials of Classic Italian Cooking by Marcella Hazan, published by Macmillan, London.

The New Italians by Charles Richards, published by Penguin.

Italian Neighbours by Tim Parks, published by Vintage.

Collins Italian Dictionary, large size, published by Collins, London.

Contatti First Course in Italian by Mariolina Freeth and Giuliana Checketts, Hodder and Stoughton, London.

501 Italian Verbs by John Colaneri and Vincent Luciani, published by Barrow's Educational Series.

BBC Italian Grammar Book by Alwena Lamping, BBC Publications.

Italy for the Gourmet Traveller by Fred Plotkin, Kyle Cathie Ltd, 122 Arlington Road, London NW1.

Italian Wines, updated every year by Gambero Rosso and the Slow Food Movement. Lists more than 13,000 wines including the top 250 *'tre bicchieres'*.

The Mediterranean Gardener by Hugo Latymer, published by Frances Lincoln in association with The Royal Botanical Gardens, Kew.

Index

Index of advertisers